Praise for Matt Lake, *Crossing the Discipleship Chasm*

Crossing the Discipleship Chasm by Matt Lake is a game-changing guide for today's churches, offering sharp insights and practical tools to revitalize discipleship in a chaotic world. Based on years of ministry experience, Lake's expert blend of timeless wisdom and innovative strategies will equip you to foster a dynamic, adaptive, resilient discipleship culture. Indispensable reading for anyone committed to deepening their approach to a discipleship that lasts, lifts up Christ, and multiplies.

—**Leonard Sweet** is author (*Designer Jesus*), professor (Drew University, George Fox University, Northwind Seminary), preacher (preachthestory.com), publisher (salishsea.press), proprietor (sanctuaryseaside.com) and founder of SpiritVenture Ministries (leonardsweet.com)

In this wise and exhilarating book, Matt Lake takes on perhaps the greatest challenge in the church today: the crisis of discipleship. Both a pastor and an adaptive leadership consultant, Matt brings a heart for the church, the boldness of an explorer, and the perspective of the innovator who has spent hours "on the balcony" learning from experiments. This book will both give words to the difficulties facing the church today and a way of approaching the challenge of discipleship that will inspire your own experimenting. It will become a go-to guide for pastors who want to recover the lost art of discipleship.

—**Tod Bolsinger** is Principal of AE Sloan Leadership and author of *Canoeing the Mountains* and *The Practicing Change Series*

Matt Lake's book is a needed innovation in the discipleship landscape. The disciple-making tools of the last decade have largely focused on more individual approaches to helping people follow Jesus. *Crossing the Discipleship Chasm* embraces a more church-centric perspective that is accessible to a wide range of churches and will help them make more and better disciples.

—**Chris Backert** is Senior Director of Fresh Expressions North America

Crossing the Discipleship Chasm was written not from abstract theory, but from years of practical study and hands-on experience. This helpful resource is full of helpful content and holds the posture of a shepherd's heart and a practitioner's mind that's rooted in people's everyday lives. If you're finding crossing the discipleship chasm to be daunting in your context, this resource will help you bridge that gap.

—**J.R. Briggs** is Founder of Kairos Partnerships and author of *The Sacred Overlap* and *Fail*

Matt Lake has offered both information and inspiration for those of us in the trenches of making disciples in a local church setting. His solid theology finds expression in practical methods of using both formal and informal means to help our church members learn better how to follow The Jesus Way. Churches of all types will find the insights in this book helpful in answering the call from Jesus to make disciples!

—**Dennis R. Wiles** is Senior Pastor of First Baptist Church in Arlington, Texas

A powerful tool for pastors, youth directors, small group leaders, ministry students, professors, and Christian college presidents! Dr. Matthew Lake's book brings clarity, insight, and hope to the complex and challenging task of making disciples in a fast-changing world. Dr. Lake's academic research and lifelong work in the trenches of local church ministry are evidence of his commitment to a thoughtful, pragmatic approach to discipleship. This work will inspire Christian leaders seeking innovative ways to reach the next generation of disciples for Christ. Dr. Lake lives and breathes the good news of Christ as he faithfully leads others in bringing people closer to God through 21st-century disciple-making.

—**Phil Greenwald** is President of Mid-America Christian University

Matt Lake has interwoven the deep riches of the historical church with the practical experience of the local congregation to discover a discipleship pathway that isn't just another church assimilation effort or plug-and-play program. With great appreciation for both the gathered and scattered church, this book guides you to embrace the multiple tensions that are necessary to help men and women become formed in the way of Jesus while embracing His mission in the world.

—**Lance Finley** is Executive Director of Churches of God, General Conference

Unlike most "plug and play" discipleship strategies, this book asks the deeper questions that can help church leaders develop an intentional, yet nuanced approach to discipleship in their setting. With his typical pastoral heart, Matt offers the humble voice of one who has trod this road with his own congregation, as together they have discovered a more "authentic, rugged discipleship."

—**Shannon Kiser** is Director of US Ministries and Training, Fresh Expressions North America

Matt Lake's approach to discipleship is refreshing! He invites us to step out of what was and navigate the changing landscape of discipleship in our world. As he leads us to reflect on where we have been, we are challenged to embrace the tensions that exist in church leadership and work together to fulfill our mission of making disciples.

—**Anne Bosarge** is Director of Leadership Strategies and Local Church Resources of the South Georgia Conference, UMC

The church might be one of the few places that longs to change lives and yet somehow believes this change can happen when one person stands up, offers a 20-minute talk, and then assumes that the people listening know what to do next and will do it. Rather than accepting this norm, Matt Lake developed a pathway in which individuals were invited to learn, discover their gifts, and put them into practice. In this much needed resource, he now offers practical wisdom and thoughtful questions designed to help you do the same. It can be used by any individual or community longing to help the church become the fullness of what Jesus intended.

—**Donna Claycomb Sokol** is pastor of Mount Vernon Place United Methodist Church in Washington, D.C.

We preachers often confuse preaching with disciple-making. There is no church without discipleship. But it is hard to make disciples, so we revert to making mere members. This accessible and inspiring book, born of Matt Lake's hard-won wisdom in parish ministry, encourages us to embrace the tensions between church-as-usual and church on-the-edge. Let's join him. Wouldn't it be more fun to multiply disciples in communion than just to manage decline?

—**Jason Byassee** is senior pastor of Timothy Eaton Memorial Church in Toronto, Ontario

Albeit clear, Jesus' command to make disciples has proven to be anything but easy in a twenty-first century (Western) church and world. In this thoughtful, practical, and timely volume, Matt Lake helps us to re-imagine what faithful, fruitful discipleship might look like today even as he encourages us to hear anew Jesus' clarion call to deny ourselves, take up the cross, and follow him.

—**Todd D. Still** is Charles J. and Eleanor McLerran DeLancey Dean & William M. Hinson Professor of Christian Scriptures at Baylor University, Truett Seminary

CROSSING THE
DISCIPLESHIP
CHASM

CROSSING THE
DISCIPLESHIP
CHASM

HOW TO TURN CROWDS INTO
PEOPLE WHO FOLLOW JESUS

MATT LAKE

invite
PRESS

Plano, Texas

I dedicate this book to all of the disciples of First Church in Williamsport, PA. Without their participation this book would not have been possible. The people of First Church not only gave me the space to dig into this work but demonstrated the courage and commitment to explore what a culture of adaptive discipleship looks like. May their example inspire many others to cross the discipleship chasm to live as disciples of Jesus.

CONTENTS

Acknowledgments   xiii

Introduction: The Tension Bridge   xv

CHAPTER ONE
Observation: Discipleship Is a Wicked Problem   1

CHAPTER TWO
Interpretation: How Might We Cross
The Discipleship Chasm?   29

CHAPTER THREE
Intervention: Embracing Discipleship Tension
To Cross The Discipleship Chasm   53

A Final Word   99

ACKNOWLEDGMENTS

A culture of adaptive discipleship requires a community in order for it to be a reality.

I am exceedingly grateful for the community that has allowed me to complete this book. I first want to thank my wife, Jennifer, for her unwavering encouragement and for being the one who advocated for me to do this work in the first place. I thank my children—Alex, Josh, and Zach—for their ongoing support and patience as this work was created.

I want to express my deep appreciation to Pastor Janet Durrwachter, who has labored with me in the creation of an adaptive discipleship approach as we worked together on the Disciple's Journey shared herein. I especially thank Janet for her work on all of the Bible study focus in this discipleship journey.

I am incredibly thankful for the support and mentorship of Tod Bolsinger in his work on adaptive leadership as it has impacted my work on discipleship in general, and for Len Sweet, who inspired me to begin this journey. I also want to thank Chris Backert for his belief in this project and for giving me the opportunity to put the ideas contained in this book into practice with a variety of churches of different backgrounds.

Much of faithful discipleship is formulated behind the scenes. I am so grateful for those who have offered much to the formation of this book behind the scenes. In particular I want to thank Ann Wilson whose editorial feedback was invaluable. I want to express appreciation to Rich Morris whose thoughts and support were crucial for the development of the book as a whole. And I want to offer my sincere gratitude to J.R. Briggs who offered some of everything to make this book a reality. You all have been more of an encouragement than you know.

Finally, and most importantly, I thank Jesus as Lord and Savior. Jesus is the reason for my passion about the importance of discipleship and is the One who has demonstrated more than anyone ever has what adaptive discipleship is really all about.

INTRODUCTION
The Tension Bridge

In the summer of 2021, two things happened that rocked my world.

One was that my family and I got to go on the trip of a lifetime that will forever hold a place in the Lake family history archives. After years of planning, saving, and prepping, and a one-year delay (thanks, Covid!), the five of us were able to take a ten-day vacation in Costa Rica. We had planned this trip as a celebration of our oldest child's graduation from high school and also the completion of my doctoral degree. It was one of those trips that was truly once in a lifetime.

Best of all—it lived up to our hopes and expectations and then some!

We experienced the beaches of the coast as well as the mountains of the interior of the country. We witnessed sloths for the first time as well as exotic birds of the rainforest. We soaked in natural hot springs and went whitewater rafting. We ate in fine restaurants and snacked on the freshest and tastiest pineapple in the world with the locals.

One of the moments that we most treasured came midway through our trip when we were able to walk among the treetops in the rainforest. You read that correctly. We were able to walk among the treetops of the rainforest. What a thrilling experience!

The experience involved exactly what the phrase suggests. In some of the rainforests of Costa Rica they have built large swinging bridges hundreds of feet off the ground, anchored by massive pillars that are dug deep into the mountains.

While walking on these swinging bridges you encounter a variety of elements, including the fog of low-lying clouds and birds flying above and below you. You feel like you are walking in the sky itself. It was both exhilarating and terrifying all at once! There was a "rush" in viewing the beauty of the rainforest from such an elevated perspective. But we also felt significant anxiety welling up within us. Taking those first few steps onto a bridge that moved (they are "swinging bridges" after all!), where you could see through the mesh walkway hundreds of feet in the air, took some nerve!

Thankfully we had a guide who walked with us each step of the way. Our guide not only offered support for the journey, but he pointed out many elements that we on our own would have missed. Thanks to him we saw toucans and egrets along with tanagers and hummingbirds. We saw yellow elder and soncoya trees. It was wonderful.

Looking back, the only reason we were able to do the near-impossible task of walking among treetops hundreds of feet off the ground was the presence of those swinging bridges, which spanned hundreds of feet across the large expanse. The conditions were such that in many spots there was no way forward from one side of the valley to the other. Something new was needed where the gaps and the difficult terrain were too much to allow someone to move forward in a normal manner. That "something new" was the creation of the swinging bridges.

The challenge of having no way forward served as a catalyst for creating a new way forward. In this case, it would not work to simply create a standard, stationary bridge. The conditions were too difficult for that approach. Nor would it work to do without a pathway of any kind. The terrain was too challenging for that approach. What was needed was a pathway that simultaneously had enough structure to allow one to make progress forward, while at the same time including an ability to be flexible responding to changing conditions. What was needed for a new way forward was a proper tension of structure and flexibility.

In very challenging conditions those swinging bridges exist in a proper tension, which creates a way forward when there is no other way. If the tension is too little, the bridges hang down too far in the gully and there is no way across. If the tension is too great, the bridges snap and no one can cross. The right amount of tension creates a way when there is otherwise no way. It is not the absence of tension that creates a way forward, but rather the right amount of tension in challenging conditions that creates that new way.

THE RIGHT AMOUNT OF TENSION CREATES A WAY WHEN THERE IS OTHERWISE NO WAY.

The second element that occurred in the summer of 2021 was something that rocked everybody's world—especially those in the "church world." In the summer of 2021 local church bodies were just starting to come to grips with the new Covid reality in which they found themselves. Many local churches had experienced at least some period of shutdown from 2020 into 2021, but as 2021 progressed, many churches were once again able to open their doors.

When they did, however, a surprise awaited them. People did not come flooding back in the ways that church leaders expected or—frankly—hoped. Estimates vary, but research suggests that depending on the age group only 30 to 70 percent of prepandemic in-person worshippers returned to an in-person worship experience when given the opportunity. While church leaders had hoped this would be a temporary anomaly, current statistics indicate a continued reality of decline after Covid compared to pre-Covid numbers.[1] Such news would have been discouraging enough had the local church had an excess of members and attendees before Covid and thus could "afford" to lose a few folks without feeling too many ill effects. However, as has been well documented, local churches have been seeing decline for a long time in their membership, particularly among denominationally affiliated congregations.[2] Thus the negative impact of the pandemic added one more challenge to a growing list of challenges already faced by local congregations, including the precipitous attendance decline, the loss of influence of the church, and decreased relevance in the culture as a whole.[3]

Not only did the pandemic create a decrease in active, in-person attendance, but it brought to the fore a host of politically charged divisions that had previously existed but had been mostly hidden. Debates over masking and vaccinations created a variety of theological responses that deeply divided previously united

---

1. Levi Lusko, *ChurchPulse Weekly* podcast, episode 99, February 2, 2022. More will be shared about the dynamics of this new reality in chapter 1. See also Justin Nortey and Michael Rotolo, "How the Pandemic Has Affected Attendance at U.S. Religious Services," Pew Research Center, March 28, 2023, https://www.pewresearch.org/religion/2023/03/28/how-the-pandemic-has-affected-attendance-at-u-s-religious-services/.

2. Jeffrey M. Jones, "U.S. Church Membership Falls Below Majority for First Time," Gallup, March 29, 2021, https://news.gallup.com/poll/341963/church-membership-falls-below-majority-first-time.aspx. Note particularly the chart "Church Membership Among U.S. Adults Now Below 50%."

3. "The Great Opportunity: The American Church in 2050," Pinetops Foundation, 2018, 17, http://www.greatopportunity.org; "Religious Landscape Study: Attendance at Religious Services," Pew Research Center, http://www.pewforum.org/religious-landscape-study/attendance-at-religious-services/.

congregations. These debates then were layered over significant racial and political differences that had already existed. Tensions began arising, it seemed, from every conceivable angle. Where there used to be only small divisions, there were now suddenly huge gaps that could not be navigated. No matter what choices were made, local church leaders seemed to be sure to alienate a significant portion of their congregations, causing many to leave. In short, there seemed to be no way to span the ever-widening gaps in this new and challenging terrain.

Given the difficult reality for local churches before the pandemic, and then the increased struggles created by Covid during the pandemic, it is no wonder that the "Great Resignation" has seen the inclusion of many pastors who have said "Enough is enough!" and chosen to seek some other profession.[4]

All of these conditions have created a terrain that local churches do not know how to navigate. In particular there are two areas of questions—separate but related—that have arisen these last few years in relation to local church ministry. One is a question of ecclesiology. Many are no longer sure what it means to be the church today when all the rules have changed. As important as this question of ecclesiological exploration is, we are not going to spend time in this book on that particular question. Many others have offered wonderful thoughts and insights around what it means to be church in this new landscape.

The other question that has been raised, and to which there seems to be much less attention given, is how to do discipleship in this new environment. The questions around discipleship appear to be almost endless in light of the challenges local churches face today.

---

4. "38% of U.S. Pastors Have Thought About Quitting Full-Time Ministry in the Past Year," Barna Group, November 16, 2021, https://www.barna.com/research/pastors-well-being/.

- How can discipleship be experienced and not just talked about?

- How do we get past a volunteer mindset to a discipleship mindset?

- How can we have a culture of healthy discipleship?

- What does effective discipleship look like?

- What does a church aligned around discipleship look like?

- In a world where no one seems to have enough time, or margin, how do we help people take discipleship seriously?

- What does it look like today to model in word and deed the ways of Jesus?

- How do we help the entire church get aligned around discipleship with so many competing demands?

- What does discipleship look like that is not simply programmatic in nature?

- What does discipleship that is challenging and compelling look like?

- How can we raise the importance of discipleship in our ministry setting?

THE CORRELATION IS CLEAR AND OBVIOUS: THE STRONGER THE DISCIPLESHIP IN A LOCAL CHURCH, THE HEALTHIER THAT LOCAL CHURCH WILL BE.

Discipleship and ecclesiology are closely linked. While there is no one "silver bullet" for church vitality, the issue of discipleship comes about as close as one can get to such a silver bullet. Inevitably healthy discipleship leads to healthy congregations and healthy ministry. The correlation is clear and obvious: the stronger the discipleship in a local church, the healthier that local church will be.

The challenge becomes, "In this adaptive age, how do we experience and foster healthy discipleship—for individuals and as corporate bodies in our churches?"

Tod Bolsinger, author of Canoeing the Mountains: Christian Leadership in Uncharted Territory, is a friend and mentor with whom I serve as a coach and consultant in his firm AE Sloan Leadership. He draws on Heifetz and Linsky's[5] helpful framework to adaptive challenges in general when he identifies the flywheel of observing, interpreting, and intervening.[6]

I have found this framework to be incredibly helpful in the local church context when considering discipleship alignment for individuals and churches. Specifically, by applying the process of observing, interpreting, and intervening to the issue of discipleship, we have discovered relevant ways of addressing many of the discipleship quandaries listed above. The cycle of observing, interpreting, and intervening simultaneously provides enough structure and flexibility to create new ways forward in discipleship within local congregations today, in ways that have not previously existed. This book offers an overview of how to apply an adaptive approach to the issue of discipleship through a series of life-giving tensions.

Too often local churches, in their anxiety, jump to quick, programmatic solutions to address the lack of discipleship happening in their settings. However, jumping to a solution that ignores the context and deeper issues of the problem will never work in the

---

5.   Ronald A Heifetz, Marty Linsky, and Alexander Grashow, The Practice of Adaptive Leadership: Tools and Tactics for Changing Your Organization and Your World. Kindle ed. (Boston: Harvard Business School Press, 2009) loc. 679-682.

6.   Tod Bolsinger, *Canoeing the Mountains: Christian Leadership in Uncharted Territory* (Downers Grove, IL: InterVarsity Press, 2015).

long run. Only after first taking time to observe and listen carefully to the key issues involved, and then discerning and interpreting what possible next steps might occur, should the actual intervention of action be taken—at least if one wants to get beyond surface-level, technical responses.

In the following pages we will explore the issue of discipleship through the three phases of observing, interpreting, and intervening. We will observe the reality of the current context of change in which we find ourselves. Then we will interpret discipleship through the tensions that exist in the swirl of change in which we find ourselves. Finally, we will determine how best to act and intervene in ways that further discipleship by embracing those tensions in new and creative ways.

As you navigate through this book, I want to invite you to embrace the tensions as they are discovered. In a culture that is so often tension-averse, it will feel odd and even uncomfortable to linger in tension rather than eliminate it. But as we saw with the swinging bridges, let the tensions be your guide into new paths forward in this difficult terrain we face. We will focus on the anchors of discipleship that come for any follower of Christ in any setting. But we will also explore how we can embrace various discipleship tensions that will empower and inspire individuals into deeper discipleship in new ways. By holding in tension the anchor points of Christian discipleship and by exploring how those anchor points may be lived out in creative ways, we will discover new ways forward to practice discipleship in the context of the church and community in which individuals find themselves.

OBSERVATION: DISCIPLESHIP IS A WICKED PROBLEM

Change is everywhere. Perhaps a more obvious statement cannot be made. Change is all around, increasing exponentially, affecting everyone and everything. No doubt that is why Bob Dylan famously sang "The times they are a-changin'" as early as 1964 in his album of the same name.

It is no secret that American society is in a time of great transition—leading to increased anxiety, chaos, and loss. Modernity has given way to postmodernity and postmodernity is giving way to "post-postmodernity"! Families come in increasingly unique shapes and sizes. Technology allows instantaneous connection with people all over the globe. Artificial intelligence is increasingly a part of everyday life. Wealth is being accumulated in unfathomed amounts by some and disproportionately lost out on by others. Living in a pandemic reality has become a new normal. The world is at an individual's fingertips on the internet. The foundations of life and culture are shaking violently, affecting every area of life. No area of society is immune.

And we certainly see the rapid, volatile pace of change occurring in the church.

This observation was brought home to me regarding discipleship in the church in an all-too-personal and embarrassingly painful way. A number of years ago, I had noticed that many people in our congregation were not taking the issue of deeper discipleship in their lives as seriously as I would hope. I could feel my anxiety rising around how to fix this problem.

I was determined, as a responsible pastor, to do something about this issue. I immediately jumped into action. I worked to create the most robust discipleship program that I could for our church. The program would be a number of weeks long, during which participants would receive significant training and teaching from me as the lead pastor. Individuals would also read books, take various spiritual inventories, and get more personalized instruction from me. I was sure it would be a great success.

At the conclusion of our final session together, I remember feeling rather satisfied with the comprehensive discipleship program I had put together. I was greeting folks on their way out that evening when one of our more mature disciples said something to me that I have never forgotten. He looked at me and said, "**Is this it?**"

I WAS GREETING FOLKS ON THEIR WAY OUT THAT EVENING WHEN ONE OF THE MEN LEAVING SAID SOMETHING TO ME THAT I HAVE NEVER FORGOTTEN. HE LOOKED AT ME AND ASKED, 'IS THIS IT?

I was rather confused by what he meant. When I asked him to explain, he shared that he felt equipped to be a good church volunteer, but not a disciple for Jesus. There it was. I had fallen into the very trap I was seeking to avoid. In that moment I realized how much church life had changed. People did not need another discipleship program to become better church volunteers. They needed a pathway of engagement in which they were equipped to live out apostolic discipleship as a way of life to impact others based on who God had made them to be. Oh, and individuals needed to be equipped this way in a time and context in which the church existed ever more on the margins of society. Not only was deeper discipleship needed, deeper discipleship was needed in the midst of a cultural reality that no seminary-trained individual was prepared to offer from a corporate church perspective.

It was then I began coming to a haunting realization: discipleship is a wicked problem. While this was a disheartening observation to make in one respect, this observation was also the catalyst for what would become an adaptive approach to discipleship for local congregations.

As any church pastor or leader will tell you, figuring out an authentic discipleship pathway for "discipleship growth" in the midst of rapid transition and turbulent times is no easy feat. It is, in fact, wicked. In a 1973 treatise, Horst Rittel and Melvin Webber described the concept of a "wicked problem," as compared to a tame, or "good," problem.[1] Wicked problems are incredibly difficult to solve due to incomplete, contradictory, changing, and morphing circumstances, where no single solution seems to exist. Elements of wicked problems include having no definitive formulation, defying any easy ways to test solutions on them, having an inexhaustible number of possible solutions or approaches, and being symptoms of other problems. Things such as education policies, public health, climate change, systemic racism, and politics increasingly fall under the category of wicked problems.

One more category can very fittingly be added to the queue of the wicked problem rubric—vital discipleship in the context of a healthy local church. Perhaps no area of society has struggled

---

1. H. W. J. Rittel and M. M. Webber, "Dilemmas in a General Theory of Planning," *Policy Sciences* 4, no. 2 (1973): 155-169, https://urbanpolicy.net/wp-content/uploads/2015/06/Rittel-Webber_1973_DilemmasInAGeneralTheoryOfPlanning.pdf.

to adjust, keep up, and thrive in the rapidly changing cultural climate more than the local church—particularly mainline denominational churches in American Western culture.

The local, denominational church in America today has struggled to remain relevant, let alone vital, in this sea of cultural change. Anecdotal examples of this reality abound around everything from lower worship attendance to the absence of youth to substantive losses of volunteers in the church. More official numbers and data reflecting this massive decline are substantive.

According to Barna researcher David Kinnaman, one in four Americans currently has no church connection at all and never did (this number has doubled in the last twenty years). Now 38 percent of the American population is post-Christian, meaning that at one time, perhaps as children, they had a church connection, but now do not. This number rises to 48 percent for those under the age of thirty.[2] David Scott summarizes this reality when he observes, "Mainline Christianity has been in numeric decline for the last half century, and within the last decade, American Christianity as a whole, including evangelical Christianity and Catholicism, has been in numeric decline."[3]

All of these numbers point to one clear reality: the decline of the local church. The real loss, however, is not a decline in numbers from an institutional perspective. The real sadness to be noted is that each one of those numbers represents a human being with whom the gospel of Jesus Christ is not being shared. Each number represents a child, a grandchild, a niece, a nephew,

---

2.   David Kinnaman, interview by Carey Nieuwhof, *The Carey Nieuwhof Leadership Podcast*, episode 24, February 23, 2015, https://careynieuwhof.com/mypodcast/.

3.   David W. Scott, "Coming to Terms with Numerical Decline in the U.S. UMC," *United Methodist Insight*, April 25, 2016, https://um-insight.net/in-the-church/umc-global-nature/coming-to-terms-with-numerical-decline/.

a friend, or a neighbor whom we love and care about who is not encountering the life-changing love, grace, and transformation of Christ. Therein is the true tragedy and reality of these numbers.

A lack of discipleship is not simply about a loss of church members. A lack of discipleship corresponds to a lack of health, vitality, and life in local churches to share in the neighborhoods and communities of which they are a part. Thus a lack of discipleship does not simply impact families, children, youth, and students who have stopped participating in the life of the church; a lack of discipleship also impacts people in each of those groups in the community who were never part of the church. In this way the church loses influence and relevance from within and from the wider culture as a whole in a downward spiral. On top of this, the lack of discipleship not only drains existing churches, it becomes a primary reason why new churches are not planted. One problem builds on another. One struggle compounds with another in which there are no simple solutions. A wicked problem of discipleship emerges.

Wicked problems are, by their very nature, multifactorial. They contain many layers of issues that must all be addressed. In this way, wicked problems are inherently dynamic—meaning they are ever-changing.

One of the more hidden realities of a wicked problem is this: in a postmodern world, many problematic issues do not happen sequentially but rather occur simultaneously. How do you then determine which issue to address first? Conflicting cultures inhabit the same space, at the same time, making it almost impossible to share information in a way that everyone can receive well.

If a church has only one primary demographic, the odds of getting that particular demographic to move beyond their own desires and comforts for the sake of connecting with those who are different from them are rather small. At the same time, in the same congregation there may be multiple cultures coexisting in the same space. The same church may easily be trying to reach mature believers, immature believers, and nonbelievers. What is meaningful and relevant to one group will not be relevant and meaningful to another. So how does one address many individuals at the same time, at the same location, who hold vastly different perspectives? For example, how does one deliver a meaningful message in a worship service around a particular passage of scripture to a gentleman who has studied scripture for sixty years of his life while at the same time speak to a young lady who has never set foot in a church facility until she decided to come with her boyfriend on that particular day? This is a wicked problem question. The same question could be asked around issues of inspiration, vision ownership, and church relevance.

DISCIPLESHIP IN MANY OF TODAY'S LOCAL CHURCHES IS A WICKED PROBLEM.

These are the types of questions that the local church now faces and must address—particularly in relation to discipleship. A local church must now try to reach and connect with people of vastly different experiences to help them grow in discipleship. Often in the same location there exist various understandings of discipleship—ranging from having no concept of what Christian discipleship is to imagining discipleship being done in any of a variety of distinct ways. Or, if the demographic is incredibly monolithic in nature, the odds of sharing in discipleship in relevant ways with those outside of the dominant culture group are long at best. These realities present imposing challenges for today's local church when it comes to discipleship, making it distinctively wicked in nature. We could ask it this way: How is today's church, in the midst of this sea of change, with so many different understandings of discipleship, and often dealing with decline, to engage in discipleship in any truly meaningful way to people of different mindsets, expectations, and circumstances?

Obviously, there are no easy answers. But there are lots of questions.

Unlike technical solutions that depend on expertise and tried-and-true methods (which have worked well in the past but not so much today because of the new landscape of reality), adaptive approaches are not threatened by ambiguity or questions. In fact, adaptive approaches are often driven by such inquiries to learn through experimentation. When it comes to discipleship, this means engaging discipleship in an ongoing, exploratory, observation-based process of asking questions, rather than applying a proficient program. It also means multiple responses can be explored simultaneously, holding them in tension with one another rather than utilizing a technical "one size fits all" approach.

For our purposes here, I want to lift up four distinct discipleship tensions. These tensions represent various continuums that people find themselves on in relation to how they engage in discipleship. Rather than exploring each element in isolation with an either/or approach, which would automatically ignore entire segments of individuals, the goal here is to embrace both elements in a carefully held tension. By then observing where people fall on the continuum of the tension, we gain insight for a new way forward to explore what more mature discipleship might look like for that individual. It does not matter whether an individual falls at the far end of one of these discipleship tensions or identifies closer to the center of each one. What matters is recognizing the tension within each continuum.

The four discipleship tensions to explore here include:

Formal vs. Informal. Formal discipleship involves many of the organized preaching, teaching, and programmatic elements used by most churches to help enforce right belief in the faith. Informal discipleship involves more relational practices such as eating together, mentoring, and serving, in which the focus is more on the practice of faith.

Going Deep vs. Exploring New. Deep discipleship opportunities focus on helping people grow in discipleship by going deeper in their faith through things such as engaging Bible studies, listening to sermons, and learning as much as they can about faith. New discipleship opportunities involve sharing the faith with people new, or newer, to the faith. The goal with new discipleship opportunities is to spread the faith.

Embracing Belief vs. Embracing Behavior. In discipleship environments focused on belief, disciples seek to transform the mind by imparting knowledge and engaging with scripture in order to accumulate more information to strengthen belief. However, in discipleship settings focused on behavior, people seek to grow in their faith journey by putting their faith into practice through what they do.

Living with a Gathered (Centralized) Mindset vs. a Sent (Decentralized) Mindset. Gathered discipleship settings focus on helping disciples grow through centralized, organized opportunities within established church facilities. The intent of gathered discipleship is to create opportunities for believers to come together to strengthen one another. In sent discipleship settings the goal is to connect with people on "their turf" outside of established church facilities in order to offer the love of Christ in relevant ways.

These types of tensions will be defined and explained more fully later on, but by naming them and beginning to ask questions about them now, we can begin to make observations that will lead to new possibilities related to discipleship engagement.

These tensions can all be observed simultaneously and on an ongoing basis. The embracing of these tensions allows for a continuous, rather than one-time, application. The beauty of this approach is that it provides an ongoing, exploratory engagement unique to each individual as he or she grows in faith. Using the deep-and-new tension as an example, perhaps an individual needs to spend more time going deep in her faith for a season in order to grow in discipleship. But then after some time perhaps she needs to reach new people with the faith in order to grow in her discipleship. The tension yields in real time the next faithful steps forward for growth in discipleship. In this way the observation of the tensions will serve as a guide by pointing to the most relevant and critical next steps of discipleship for individuals no matter where they find themselves on the discipleship journey.

The importance of taking the time to do some careful observation cannot be overstated. In times of distress, particularly in church environments experiencing distress, our anxiety causes us to want to immediately react. In the case of discipleship, our temptation is to quickly apply an efficient discipleship program, which is a technical response. However, without taking the time to properly observe, we will not know where people individually are in their discipleship journeys nor in what areas of discipleship they need to grow. The default is to apply some discipleship program that has gotten good reviews, but realistically this is not relevant to where many people are in their discipleship development. Then because the discipleship program is not relevant to many of the individuals going through the program, no real maturing of discipleship occurs. The pastor may feel good for having attempted to address "the discipleship problem," but the effort does not foster a culture of discipleship vitality. Many discipleship programs seek to address discipleship from a "one size fits all" approach, while ignoring the swirl of massive change currently affecting every church. The application of one prescribed program to meet all discipleship needs is a technical approach. Such a technical approach may have worked fifty years ago. But today these technical solutions to discipleship almost always miss the mark.

Thus, as tempting as it is to immediately do something to fix our discipleship brokenness, we must first take some time to really observe the wicked nature of the discipleship problem we face. We do this because we cannot navigate what we cannot name. Without taking time to do some serious observation, we run the risk of offering an unhelpful activity rather than a relevant response.

OBSERVATION: A WICKED PROBLEM REQUIRES AN ADAPTIVE SOLUTION

The statistics already cited highlight the wicked nature of what I like to call "multiplying discipleship" (that is, discipleship in one individual or group that ultimately leads to discipleship in other individuals or groups). Part of that wicked reality is this: no simple, or technical, solution exists for how to easily foster multiplying discipleship.

Multiplying discipleship has a wide variety of factors working against it in the context of today's local churches. In fact, it is a challenge to even identify all of these realities, let alone adequately address them to help the church again find its discipleship footing. To explore the depth of the problem, many simultaneous factors must be named. Then to evaluate we must spend some time doing careful discipleship observation in our current reality.

OBSERVING SPECIFIC BARRIERS TO CROSSING THE DISCIPLESHIP CHASM

One: Cultural Upheaval

For centuries, the religious landscape of the American church was dominated by the scientific, modern mindset of the Enlightenment. Lesslie Newbigin once posed the issue this way, which I have found to be helpful: "How can we move from the place where we explain the gospel in terms of our modern scientific worldview to the place where we explain our modern scientific worldview from the point of view of the gospel?"[4]

There was a time when local churches were central in communities, with the rest of the community literally built around them. This reality has changed. Many local churches fail to realize their context has changed and that their voice is marginal at best. I increasingly find myself working with churches in downtown areas that were once thriving with the church in the middle of all the vitality. Many of these churches, however, now have no one from the church living within a multimile radius of the building. As a result, the voice of these local churches is increasingly lost because they do not know the realities of the very neighbor-

---

4.   Lesslie Newbigin, *Foolishness to the Greeks: The Gospel and Western Culture* (Grand Rapids, MI: William B. Eerdmans, 1986), 22.

hoods that they inhabit. They no longer have the ability to speak or minister in relevant ways as the community and culture around them changes. The church facility may inhabit a space in the community, but many times these same churches have lost their incarnational presence because all of their members now drive in for worship on Sundays. It is hard to know how to minister in a changing context if one is not incarnationally present to change within that cultural context.

Because of its massive impact on culture, few elements illustrate the high level of change for all of culture more than technology. In a world where individuals can now hold the world in the palm of their hand through technology, local churches face the challenge of seeking to remain relevant. How is the church to offer a faithful and countercultural witness with the endless individual choices that are at one's fingertips on their phone? What does it mean to share in meaningful discipleship in a world where there are apps for everything from locating the nearest Thai food restaurant to listening to one's favorite artist? This is a world and culture that did not exist just a few decades ago. This adaptive shift in culture is massive. The local church must not only be aware of such a shift but learn to navigate it in such a way as to foster vibrant discipleship within the midst of it.

Two: Irrelevant Measurements

A while back I was chatting with a colleague about possible reasons why we were not seeing multiplying discipleship occurring in so many churches. My colleague made an interesting statement. He said matter-of-factly, "Churches are measuring the wrong things." When I asked what he meant, he said, "Churches are measuring attendance and cash instead of leaders and apprentices.

It is easy to get a crowd for worship but that does not translate to deep discipleship practices." Ever since he said that, I have found myself observing this reality over and over. Many churches still hold Sunday worship. Many churches know how to count worship attendance and money from the offerings. But I know of very few churches that are so intentional about their discipleship development that they count numbers of mentors and apprentices involved in discipleship.

When the focus is on metrics such as worship attendance and budgets, the mindset becomes entirely internally focused rather than externally focused. I once heard it described as a focus on seating capacity rather than sending capacity. Such an internal focus makes the sending of disciples a difficult orientation to live into.

On another occasion, a very good friend of mine made the observation that for the last few generations, the focus in churches has been on membership rather than discipleship. As a result, we are reaping what we have sown—good members rather than effective disciples. Members focus on institutional maintenance. Disciples focus on practices oriented toward the living out and sharing of the Kingdom of God in such a way as to help others come to embrace life and faith in Jesus Christ. The difference between member and disciple is vast.

The example modeled by Jesus with His disciples reveals a focus on practices such as apprenticeship so that discipleship can truly occur, rather than the adherence to particular membership vows. The discipleship goal is to emulate the master, in this case Jesus, not simply know information about the master. Jesus began a viral movement through the practice of apprenticing His disciples through relationship, dialogue, service, and sharing life together. Thus disciples today must also embody the same types of practices in order to create new disciples and foster multiplying discipleship.

Unless local churches draw people to Christ and help them to live like Christ, all the church facilities and ministry programs in the world will be for naught. This is why irrelevant measurements yield irrelevant discipleship. However, when we lose our discipleship imagination the only default metrics we know to turn to for some form of evaluation are the number of attendees, the condition of our facilities, and the amount of cash in the bank account.

Three: Institutional Preservation

When local churches begin to experience decline—which the vast majority of local churches in the Western culture are experiencing—the default becomes surviving over thriving. This focus on survival turns to keeping the doors open and doing just enough to stay alive. In other words, institutional preservation becomes the primary goal.

If you look back into the origins of so many local churches, it's amazing how many began with a strong, missional impulse in which discipleship involved missional formation. Yet over time, as churches begin to decline, that focus on a discipleship of reaching others transitions to a mindset of serving themselves. In this way discipleship is directed toward building maintenance rather than relational maintenance with those who may not know the love of Christ. The focus shifts from community pain points to address to in-house matters. In this way the norm for so many local churches becomes caring for church buildings and members over new people.

When this discipleship shift becomes the reality for a church, that church has effectively taken the first step toward ensuring no more new generations of disciples are reached. At the same time, more and more churches focus on training shepherds and teachers to care for and edify those in the institutional church, but neglect investing in apostles and evangelists to be sent to those outside the church in an incarnational way. This institutional focus creates a lack of generative life and energy essential to viral discipleship by failing to encounter new people where they might be. How ironic in these instances that so many churches that originated with a discipleship focused on sharing the incarnational presence of Jesus with new people in the community now offer forms of programmatic discipleship focused on self-preservation.

Four: Passive Christian Spirituality

Throughout my life I have been influenced by the Presbyterians (from birth to my teen years), Brethren in Christ (my college years), and Methodists (overlapping in upper teens and graduate study years)—not to mention many wonderful friends from other faith traditions. One element common to each of these religious movements in history is that each one had a person of great significance and influence (whether Calvin, Engle, or Wesley) who was abundantly full of passion for the faith and life in Jesus Christ. These influencers were so captivated by the passion of the faith they could not hold back their enthusiasm. Their passion was exuberant!

Yet in so many local churches today in the Western culture, the word "passionate" is about the last word that would describe their discipleship reality. If part of discipleship is about emulating the ways and practices of Jesus, then many churches have lost that sense of discipleship as they have lost their passion for Jesus.

What once may have been a raging fire of passion in Christian formation has dwindled to a few sparks at best. Rarely is discipleship marked by passion and excitement. The reality is that no one wants to belong to a church, or anything else for that matter, if it is devoid of passion and purpose that speaks into one's life. In an effort to combat people refusing to engage in discipleship the local church has often responded by lowering the challenges of discipleship. But this is the wrong response. People will rise up and respond to challenges put before them if they are filled with passion and see the importance and relevance of a life of discipleship. The issue is not lowering the standards of discipleship but reclaiming the passion behind it.

Five: Culture of Instant Gratification

This particular barrier to discipleship is one of the most obvious. In a world of fast food, microwaves, instant text messaging, electronic banking, online shopping, and access to almost endless information with the click of a button or swipe of the finger, the willingness to be patient is an increasingly lost art.

Patience is barely understood as a concept today, let alone practiced. For desperate, declining churches, or for church plants that must produce results before their grant runs out or before they must answer to the authorities to whom they are accountable, patience seems impossible. But the practices necessary for viral discipleship take time to be learned, fostered, embodied, and mastered. Much like an airplane accelerating down a runway before taking off to great heights, or a pot of homemade stew that must simmer all day before being consumed, viral discipleship takes time before someone experiences the best results.

One of the reasons the early church was able to remain resilient in the face of threats, persecution, and lack of resources was the extensive time and patience given to developing a robust discipleship in individuals. Early students of the faith were mentored over the course of years (yes, years! not weeks or months) in knowledge and practice as well. In other words, discipleship was a patient lifestyle learned.

Six: Stability Focus

Two bumper stickers that I have encountered capture the essence of people's perspective on change. One bumper sticker said, "Change is good. You go first." The other said, "Change is good. Unless it happens." While individuals—and churches—may know that change is needed, they still offer strong resistance to it. Whether it is fear of the unknown or the loss of what has been comfortable, human beings find change to be challenging.

As a result, the default response is to cling to stability, which means the status quo. Even when that status quo is leading into decline, the resistance to change often carries the day. Usually the larger the institution, the more resistance there is to change and the stronger push there is to maintain order and stability. Messiness is to be avoided. I grew up in a denomination in which numerous, annual statistical reports were the norm rather than engagement in experimental endeavors.

And yet the Church is meant to be a living and breathing entity. Scripture even refers to the people of God as the "body" of Christ (Ephesians 4:15-16; Colossians 3:15). Bodies are meant to move, grow, adapt, respond. All of these elements require change.

Too much control, management, or institutionalization, far from fostering life in the church, kills the Church. Rainforests, as we experienced firsthand on our trip to Costa Rica, are areas of tremendous beauty, vitality, and messiness. Overgrown trees, tons of varieties of species of animals, dense carpets of moss, and more species of insects than can be counted exist in that ecosystem. It is not tidy. It is not managed in an orderly fashion.

Many churches today, particularly from mainline denominations, are driven more by administration than by exploration. Thus it would seem there is more of a desire for stability than for experimentation. Even though Jesus says the Holy Spirit will blow where it will (John 3:8), many churches today still seem bent on trying to dictate exactly where that wind will blow. This concept applies not only to the life of the church in a general manner but also when it comes to the practice and exploration of deeper discipleship.

Seven: Retreating versus Exploring

As a lead pastor, one of the more frustrating and time-consuming tasks I have encountered in ministry has been the process of replacing staff or volunteers when they leave a position. For many years, every time one of these transitions comes up I found a part of myself resisting and trying to hold on to what had been—even when the change might be good for the individual, the church, or both! Why? Because I did not look forward to the time and effort it would take to explore new candidates—even if they looked like they could do an amazing job. Even if a new person would bring many new benefits, I would find myself holding on to what was familiar with the person who had been in the role. The familiarity of retreating back to what I knew was more comfortable than exploring forward in new ways. While I still struggle with transitions when they come, a trusted mentor helped me to reframe these transitions as opportunities. He literally told me, "Every transition is an opportunity." And he was right! Any time a trusted staff person needs to transition, there is a sense of sadness and loss. But these losses are always softened by the new gifts the new person brings to move forward.

In church environments the desire to retreat frequently overrides the need to explore moving forward. Of all organizations, the church ought to be on the front end of leading change and fostering creativity. Led by the Holy Spirit and in service to the Creator of all, the church is best equipped to explore into the future on a continual basis. However, those in the church know that the opposite is most often what is encountered. When today's church faces new challenges and changes from how it has always been, it often reacts negatively instead of engaging positively. Rather than the transition being viewed as an opportunity for something new, it is taken as a mourning of what has been lost.

The impact of this type of mindset on discipleship is significant. Until churches can reclaim an exploration of discipleship along with the possibilities of where such discipleship may take the churches and individuals, those churches and individuals will be limited in their impact for the Kingdom. In the book of Acts, the original apostles were marked in their discipleship by a spirit of pioneering and exploring into a world that did not know the gospel. In a culture that is increasingly unfamiliar with the gospel, such a posture of discipleship is once again needed.

Observing these seven obstacles to multiplying discipleship illustrates the wicked, complex nature of the problem of fostering multiplying discipleship in local churches. This reality highlights why a strictly technical, programmatic approach to discipleship—which is what most local churches seek to apply—so often fails. Technical approaches work when expertise is needed to address one particular issue. But when one issue is simultaneously impacted by a plethora of obstacles, technical solutions can no longer adequately address the problem.

This observation stage allows for a fuller understanding of the scope of the discipleship problem. Observation allows us to navigate the challenges before us by being keenly aware of them. However, taking time to observe the nature of the discipleship problem does more than highlight the magnitude of the problem. Observation also provides the necessary clues for navigating forward in an adaptive manner. In this way, observation points to signs of hope even in the midst of the most daunting circumstances.

FINDING HOPE FOR CROSSING THE DISCIPESHIP CHASM
OBSERVE: AN OLD/NEW APPROACH

Historically, the church has addressed the problem of a lack of discipleship through various ideations. These attempts can be categorized as having "curriculum-esque" tendencies focused upon both teaching (directed toward belief formation) and practice (directed toward generation of life in self and others). In the early church, the catechesis was used to concentrate on this rigorous teaching and practice in order to instill formative and generative elements of multiplying discipleship.[5] In other movements, such as the Wesleyan movement, individuals such as John Wesley came up with what can be viewed as contemporized forms of curricula.

---

5. For a helpful overview of the intensity of the catechesis process please see Alan Kreider, *The Patient Ferment of the Early Church*, particularly chapters 4–6.

For example, Wesley's Sermons and the Articles of Religion provided information for sound teaching while also placing emphasis on particular practices such as proclaiming the gospel, leading others to Christ, Christian conferencing, and being sent to people who did not yet know the gospel. The catechesis of the early church and the Wesleyan movement were not shared in forms of curriculum as we often think of today. But they fulfilled the role of what curricula can offer—both then and now. Observing these early movements, we discover the emergence of vital discipleship that was marked by embracing the tension of both formative as well as generative realities.

Today, many local churches have no discipleship pathway or corporate intentionality to foster discipleship in the life of the congregation. For those churches that do have some type of discipleship pathway, the reality is that the vast majority of these approaches present formative teaching in a one-dimensional, information-only approach without considering the context of an increasingly post-Christian culture. The net result is often a series of discipleship programs that focus on creating committed volunteers within the church rather than preparing and sending laity to explore multiplying discipleship outside the church. Additionally, these discipleship programs focus predominantly on discipleship in the most limited formational sense only, leading only to discipleship as information consumption rather than practice. Such one-dimensional approaches rarely make much of an impact in the face of the wicked discipleship problem. But if churches today can once again embrace the model of earlier church movements by fostering the tension between formative and generative realities, then there is hope for reclaiming healthy discipleship that once again impacts the world.

OBSERVE: PROPER FORMATION TAKES TIME

When my family and I embarked on that magical trip to Costa Rica, we did not simply wake up the morning of our departure date and say, "Let's go to Costa Rica today." The reality was that we had spent months and months preparing for that trip. We had saved money, discussed the best dates to go, talked with others who had gone there, consulted a travel agent, googled tons of reviews, talked with our kids about what they wanted to do, secured passports, planned multiple excursions, and mapped out an extensive itinerary. It took a lot of planning, a lot of preparation, and a lot of time. But all the planning made the execution of the trip that much more meaningful and impactful. The formation that occurred in organizing the information for the trip best prepared us when it came time to live out the trip. Had we simply flown to Costa Rica with no plan or preparation or awareness of information related to Costa Rica, our trip would have been much less rich in meaning and practice. Conversely, had we only studied up on Costa Rica and learned all about it by gathering information but never actually going on the trip, we would have also missed out on a powerful experience. Both the information and the practice were necessary for the best trip. Both the formation found in the preparation and the generation of new life found in the practices of the trip were required for the trip to reach its maximum impact.

When it comes to discipleship, proper formation takes time. While many discipleship plans do include specific time spent in study and focus, the time frames often remain relatively short. Some discipleship plans are twelve weeks long. Others are half that amount of time. In these types of pathways, time is given to share information, but that time is limited. In embracing quick discipleship paths, churches adopt a posture of immediacy that does not often lead to deep formation. It is the discipleship equivalent of consuming a can of soup heated up in the microwave versus a homemade stew that has been slowly cooking in the Crock-Pot all day.

Because many contemporary discipleship pathways have a shorter time of instruction, the most they can do is focus on presenting information rather than engaging in the practices of formation. Practices take time to master. One must observe and learn, but then also experiment, evaluate, learn, relearn, and embody the practices of the faith. Such practice simply takes time.

As a child I learned to play the piano. Every week I would spend thirty minutes with my piano teacher learning the theoretical side of music . . . including arpeggios, sharps, flats, sixteenth notes, dotted half notes, and whole rests. This information was needed to play the piano. But I would then spend many hours outside of that lesson time, on my own, practicing the music over and over again until I learned how to correctly implement the theory in each song I played. Much more time was spent practicing and implementing the theory in the music than just learning about the music.

Take a look at any discipleship pathways you may be aware of—either in your own church or in another church you're familiar with. The vast majority of discipleship pathways that exist contain up to 70 percent or even 90 percent information. This reality makes sense since most discipleship pathways are only a few months (at best) long. Most are only weeks long. With such short time frames, there is only time for information without getting into practices of generation. Such a focus makes it easy to think that discipleship can be lived out simply by being aware of the necessary information. Such an approach is the discipleship equivalent to watching a two-minute video on how to surf and thinking that by consuming the information of the video, you are suddenly able to go out and properly ride a surfboard on any wave that comes your way. Of course, any sane person knows this is most certainly not how it works!

OBSERVE: AN ORIENTATION OUTWARD

Common to many discipleship plans is also an internal/institutional church focus when it comes to living as a disciple. Given that many pathways are information-heavy, when practices are suggested, they are nearly always offered with a focus within the institutional church rather than beyond it. *Ideal discipleship is often defined as sharing in regular worship, participating in a small group of some kind, learning in an ongoing Bible study, and then serving somewhere to fill a need (usually some church volunteer or outreach program).* Examine the curriculum for almost any discipleship pathway and you will discover that a primary goal is to help individuals find their place to serve as volunteers somewhere in the established church facility. Similarly, you will discover that the key metrics for discipleship are elements such as worship attendance, giving, and Bible study opportunities, which all relate to the institutional church. Repeatedly, these focal points in the church are the gold standard by which mature disciples are measured. This kind of discipleship has primarily an "in-church" focus when it speaks of the importance of community, learning, and serving. Yet such a discipleship focus leads to an obvious problem: the lack of connection and interaction with non-Christians.

With this observation it becomes clear that discipleship for today's churches must include a focus beyond the institutional church if such discipleship is going to have an impact in the lives of others. Thus some helpful questions to ask in light of this observation would be: How might discipleship be approached in a way that fosters interaction and service beyond that of an institutional church volunteer? What might this begin to look like?

OBSERVE: MORE APOSTOLIC PRACTICES

The lack of apostolic practices in many discipleship pathways is evident. Practices related to ongoing mentoring, missional discipleship, recruitment to the Way (of Christ), fasting, extended catechesis, the priesthood of all believers, testimony sharing, radical hospitality, extravagant generosity, engagement with the wider community, planting of new faith communities, sacrificial living, contextual living, and extended praying are all conspicuously absent from nearly all discipleship plans. If some of these primary practices—which both form deeper discipleship in individuals and simultaneously reach out to individuals beyond the institutional church—are not present in a discipleship pathway, then eventually it will be impossible for local churches to experience growth or multiplication. But if such apostolic practices are incorporated, then the odds of individual discipleship impacting others, especially non-Christians, dramatically rises because the focus moves beyond a solely insular, internal perspective.

In these ways, careful observation can lead to clarifying questions, which can begin to give us new direction in the quagmire of the wicked reality of discipleship challenges faced by local churches. *If you pause right now, what observations can you make in your current setting? As you consider those observations carefully, what helpful questions do these observations raise? What practices are missing? What practices need to be employed?* The better we observe, the better questions we can ask . . . and the more clarity we can gain to move forward in new ways.

When the early church observed and asked what was needed to foster true discipleship in a world and culture that did not know the gospel, it did not embrace an either/or approach. The early church did not focus just on formative teaching or generative practices. It embraced both.

THE EARLY CHURCH DID NOT FOCUS JUST ON TEACHING OR PRACTICES TO FOSTER DISCIPLESHIP. IT FOCUSED ON BOTH IN A HOLY TENSION.

Christians know they are forming rightly when formation and generative practices are the result. While many churches foster elements of formation, many need more focus on practices of generation. Both are needed because formation and generation feed seamlessly off each other. There is a holy tension of ebb and flow, along with a simultaneous filling and releasing as modeled in the dance found in the Trinitarian relationships.

This holy, beautiful discipleship tension is fueled by careful, nonrushed observation and the questions such observation raises, questions that inform helpful interpretation. It is to more interpretation that we now turn.

OBSERVATION QUESTIONS AND ANSWERS

1. Using only "I see" statements, describe where you are seeing discipleship thrive in your setting. Describe where it is not. Be explicit. Do not feel pressure to solve any disciple-

ship issues yet. Take time to observe the issues. We cannot navigate what we cannot name.

2. Describe the discipleship pathway in your local setting. Do you have one? If so, what does it cover? What does it not cover?

3. What do you mean by "discipleship"? Give a clear definition for all to agree upon.

4. Name the cultural factors in your setting making discipleship difficult.

5. What metrics are you currently using to evaluate discipleship? Are there additional metrics you can use?

6. Do disciples in your setting serve in the church? out of the church? in volunteer roles? as leaders?

7. Is there a sense of passion connected with the discipleship occurring in your setting?

8. Is discipleship prioritized in your setting? What ongoing discipleship efforts exist?

9. Are lives being transformed as a result of deeper discipleship?

10. Discipleship faces many simultaneous challenges in local churches. Name the top three discipleship challenges in your setting. Prioritize them from most pressing to least pressing. Why did you rank the challenges as you did?

11. What areas of discipleship are individuals in your setting strongest in? In which areas are they needing the most growth?

12. Is discipleship viewed as a programmatic focus in your church among many other ministry programs? Or as part of the overall culture of your church? Explain.

13. Do you foster a "Crock-Pot" or "microwave" approach to discipleship in your setting?

14. Choose three adjectives to best describe the discipleship culture in your setting. Make sure you can back up your response by saying, "Because I see . . ."

15. What technical approaches to discipleship are you offering?

16. What adaptive approaches to discipleship are you offering?

17. Take time to record your answers to the previous questions. Create as complete a discipleship profile as you can for your setting. Take time to discuss this profile with your governance board, key staff, and key leaders. Pray on it. Seek alignment. Be clear on the state of discipleship in your setting.

INTERPRETATION: HOW MIGHT WE CROSS THE DISCIPLESHIP CHASM?

"This is the way; walk in it."
—Isaiah 30:21

So far attention has been given to taking the time needed to observe the realities needed for healthy discipleship to occur. This focus on observation in relation to discipleship will continue (in fact it never really stops), but we must do more than observe. We must look at what has been observed and begin to make helpful interpretations from the observations which will eventually lead to experimenting with new ways forward that are effective.

One of the immediate observations made so far has been that discipleship is increasingly a wicked problem requiring an adaptive, not a technical, approach. This means that healthy approaches to discipleship will require forms of experimentation, a both/and approach rather than an either/or approach, and that technical solutions alone stand little chance of resulting in long-term success. In light of these realities, we can seek to make interpretations to eventually prototype and implement over time. Utilizing the phrase "How might we . . ." is a particularly helpful way of interpreting our way forward. So, for example, we could go through each observation above and start to ask interpretive question such as:

- How might we foster healthy discipleship in light of cultural upheaval?

- How might we foster discipleship in a way that encourages exploration into the world?

- How might we advocate for a more patient discipleship in a world of instant gratification?

- How might we develop a discipleship approach beyond our own desires?

These interpretive questions have then led me to a host of other interpretive questions. Specifically, I have wondered and wrestled with questions such as:

- How might we raise up mature disciples, recognizing that much of what we have been doing to raise up such disciples is not working?

- How might we offer a discipleship approach that fosters discipleship from more than one angle?

- How might we encourage discipleship holding together the tension of formation and generation at the same time?

- How might we foster a more organic approach to discipleship that is not so programmatic in nature?

- How might we help people engage discipleship in light of cultural realities?

- How might we live into discipleship in a way that affirms who we are while simultaneously challenging us beyond our own comfort limits?

Based on what you have observed in regards to discipleship in your setting, what interpretive questions most resonate with you? Which ones would you add?

These types of interpretive questions do not have premade manuals with the answers already produced for you. They require imagination, exploration, experimentation, and eventually intervention.

But how do we even know what experiments to attempt?

In my own life I have noticed that careful observation of life in general, across various disciplines, often yields inspiration for how best to make helpful interpretations in areas unrelated to those disciplines—such as in the arena of discipleship.

By exploring or holding different fields in tension, I have found interpretive clues for moving forward in new ways, even in the midst of the overwhelming force of wicked problems. I will confess that this is something that I personally enjoy doing. I view it almost like searching for hidden treasures of wisdom and possibility in places we may not expect to find them. There is something about cross-referencing apparently unrelated elements and holding those disciplines in tension that unlocks our imaginations to provide pathways forward where previously there were none. (Perhaps this is why I chose to study semiotics—the study of the use of symbolic communication to interpret signs of the times— in a doctoral program some years ago with Dr. Leonard Sweet at Portland Seminary. I would highly recommend such a study opportunity to anyone who can pursue it! But you do not need to have a degree in semiotics to make interpretive connections.)

If you will bear with me a few moments, let me lift up some examples of what I am talking about and how holding different disciplines in tension with one another might work for new interpretations of vital discipleship today. I invite you to stay with me on this for a bit as we keep in the back of our mind all of the interpretive questions previously raised.

First, let me lift up the discipline of history.

Even though experiencing multiplying discipleship today exists as a wicked problem to overcome, the reality is that each age has faced discipleship challenges. We should not be so egocentric as to assume that the challenge of flourishing discipleship in the church is completely unique to us. As Ecclesiastes 1:9 reminds us, there is nothing new under the sun. Therefore, when I need guidance on how best to move forward, I have found that taking time to look back in history has often proven beneficial to search for clues that might speak to moving forward in our situation today.

While looking back in history, I have found two time periods in particular to be helpful in finding clues for healthy discipleship. Following is a brief summary of both of those time periods, involving both the early church and the Wesleyan movement begun by John Wesley in the eighteenth and nineteenth centuries. In both instances there were leaders and influencers who were able to observe well the context they were in and then make helpful interpretations in light of the discipleship challenges they were facing.

Interpretation: What clues do the birth of the church in the first centuries and the Wesleyan movement in America in the eighteenth and nineteenth centuries provide for today's discipleship?

As these two time periods are compared, it becomes clear how particular similarities of discipleship in both times helped foster an entire movement of discipleship. In each movement there existed tension—with a focus on both formative components (marked by the Ephesians 4:11 offices of teachers, shepherds, and prophets) and generative components (marked by the Ephesians 4:11 offices of apostles and evangelists). Such components do not exist in a vacuum, where one is fundamentally separate from the other, but rather exist in a holy tension of give and take, where one makes the other better. The formational elements of teaching allow for a sense of consistency and clarity among all disciples anywhere, while the generative practices of living allow discipleship to grow organically, creatively, and imaginatively among nonbelievers in whatever new environments disciples find themselves.

SEARCHING FOR DISCIPLESHIP CLUES FROM THE EARLY CHURCH

In the early church, the power of the formative community, with its focus upon teaching, shepherding, and prophesying, was evident.[1] Teaching was a key ingredient in the discipleship culture of the early Christians as they formed a new way of living based on agreed-upon teaching known as catechesis. In this way, the living out that would occur was grounded in the truths of the teaching offered.

In addition to teaching, formation through shepherding in worshipping communities was viewed as essential for the church's mission of discipleship. The worship that was led by those with shepherding gifts fostered allegiance and identity in the living out of the faith.

Finally, early Christians were anchored to live discipleship-modeling faith in Christ through a prophetic focus on the truth of Jesus. In particular, Jesus's Sermon on the Mount served as prophetic fuel for what a life of discipleship was meant to look like in a countercultural manner. The prophetic focus of early Christians

---

1. In relation to this discussion I would recommend Alan Kreider's *The Patient Ferment of the Early Church* and Alan Hirsch's *The Forgotten Ways*, focused on the five offices of apostles, prophets, evangelists, shepherds, and teachers.

helped them to remain anchored in lives distinct from the world around them.

At the same time, the offices of apostleship and evangelism were just as important in the early church as the offices of the formative community, offering new life through a focus on generation. Apostles were, in the model of the original twelve disciples of Jesus in scripture, those missionaries on the frontiers doing what could only be explained as the work of God. They did what Jesus had done, by going where Jesus had gone and beyond. They were true pioneers of the faith who had to figure out how to live the gospel of Jesus Christ in a world that did not know the gospel—no matter what sacrifice it cost them. This sacrificial, on-the-ground, meeting-people-where-they-were approach fostered new life among nonbelievers.

Evangelists also played a crucial part in the multiplying discipleship of the early church. Evangelists were essentially recruiters to the cause and good news of Christ, able to share the gospel in such a way that others could receive it well. If apostles had to figure out how to pioneer the faith in relevant ways to the surrounding culture through their living, evangelists had to figure out how to communicate the gospel in effective ways. Their orientation was to those not already in the life of the church. Thus they were constantly on the go to share the faith in new locations beyond the established Christian community.

Notice that all five offices—teachers, shepherds, prophets, apostles, and evangelists—working together created a formative and generative tension through which healthy discipleship could occur. This tension was occurring in a culture that did not know the gospel. This tension-filled reality would not prove to be an anomaly.

SEARCHING FOR DISCIPLESHIP CLUES FROM A HISTORICAL MOVEMENT

I was blessed to have my own faith formation heavily influenced by what I learned in the Wesleyan tradition. As in the early church, teaching, shepherding, and prophecy played prevalent roles in the Wesleyan tradition. Teaching was based on such doctrinal materials as the Articles of Religion, the Confession of Faith, the General Rules, and Wesley's Sermons and Notes. Shepherding came through intentional religious gatherings, including both larger and smaller assemblies. Sometimes formation occurred through field preaching to thousands and sometimes formation occurred in small groups often called religious societies or band meetings.

The Wesleyan movement lived into the prophetic office by offering clear declarations of truth that set them apart from other religions. Some of those formational, prophetic distinctions included a commitment to orthodoxy, repenting and believing in the gospel as the only way to heaven, justification through grace alone, and living into that justification. At the same time, some of the generative prophetic distinctions for Wesley included serving the broken, lost, poor, and hurting while sharing the good news.

The Wesleyan movement gained momentum because it not only lived into the formational offices of teaching, shepherding, and prophesying, it embraced the tension that came with practicing the generative offices of apostles and evangelists as well. John Wesley himself began as the primary apostle and evangelist in the Methodist movement. Wesley felt compelled during his life to disregard parish boundaries and normal parish protocol in his attempts to fulfill God's commission to him to preach the gospel to everyone that he could. It was from this apostolic mindset that innovative (at the time) approaches such as the use of circuit riders and itinerant preachers would rise to carry the gospel to the fringes of society.

Evangelism also played a strong role in Wesley's renewal movement. Over time the Wesleyan revival swept across all of England, into Wales, Scotland, and Ireland, and eventually to North America. Why? Because inherent in the movement was a commitment to going "on" and "out" to those who did not yet know the good news of the love of Jesus. That missional impulse would drive the Wesleyan movement to places other movements had not reached.

SEARCHING FOR DISCIPLESHIP CLUES FOR TODAY'S CHURCH

In looking at both of these faith movements in history, what clues can be noticed? We see that in both the early church movement and the Wesleyan movement, the active presence of the offices of apostles, prophets, evangelists, shepherds, and teachers was moving in a synergistic tension between formative and generative discipleship. This tension helped the early disciples and individuals such as Wesley navigate well their own cultural contexts (both of which involved cultures that were not familiar with the gospel) by finding effective ways to foster discipleship. In other words, the synergistic tension involving formation and generation helped those leaders to interpret the best steps to take in their context so that healthy discipleship could flourish.

Next, let me lift up the academic discipline of cognitive psychology.

I was struck some years ago by the work of Karl Duncker, who proposed one of the most famous hypothetical problems in all of cognitive psychology.

The problem is described this way:

Suppose you are a doctor faced with a patient who has a malignant tumor in his stomach. It is impossible to operate on the patient, but unless the tumor is destroyed the patient will die. There is a kind of ray that can be used to destroy the tumor. If the rays reach the tumor all at once at a sufficiently high intensity, the tumor will be destroyed. Unfortunately, at this intensity the healthy tissue that the rays pass through on the way to the tumor will also be destroyed. At lower intensities the rays are harmless to healthy tissue, but they will not affect the tumor either. What type of procedure might be used to destroy the tumor with the rays, and at the same time avoid destroying the healthy tissue?[2]

Many medical students and philosophers have wrestled to figure out the solution. The answer is that you (the doctor) could direct multiple low-intensity rays at the tumor from different directions, leaving healthy tissue intact, but converging at the tumor site with enough collective intensity to destroy it. In addressing the issue from a number of vantage points in a converging manner, the solution emerges.

A RIGHT TENSION CAN CREATE A WAY WHERE THERE WAS NO WAY BEFORE.

Notice in this illustration, the "answer" ultimately comes from the tension between the inability to operate on the patient and the need to still save the patient's life. While the tension creates a challenge to overcome, the tension also leads to an interpretation that leads to a new way forward that has not previously been tried. Remember the opening illustration in this book. How was it that the challenge of traversing the gap in the Costa Rica

---

2. M. L. Gick and K. J. Holyoak, "Analogical Problem Solving," *Cognitive Psychology* 12 (1980): 306–55.

rainforest was overcome? By harnessing a right tension with the suspension of the swinging bridge. A right tension can create a way where there was no way before.

At the same time, from the example of the Duncker illustration, we see that the solution comes from a multifaceted approach. Might this provide another clue when it comes to fostering healthy multiplying discipleship in congregations—such as applying multiple discipleship approaches, for instance both formational and generative? Or applying different levels of intensity of discipleship from different angles? Or simply trying a brand new approach?

Let me suggest a final discipline to hold in tension with the exploration of history and cognitive psychology: marketing and advertising.

When you are able, take a few moments to view two shoe commercials from two different eras.

The first commercial is an advertisement for selling Kinney shoes in 1976 using actor Ken Berry as the primary "seller" of the shoes. You can watch this commercial at this link:

https://www.youtube.com/watch?v=h8aAFHhaIKc

Compare that commercial with this 2023 Nike "Beyond" commercial:

https://www.youtube.com/watch?v=8_6hjIAF5Ws

What differences did you notice?

While there are many to note, I will observe just a few here for us to consider. Remember, both commercials have the same goal, which is to sell shoes. But how they did this in 1976 compared to 2023 is very different. The 1976 commercial focused on high choreography with a large group, patriotic themes, a celebrated actor of the day, and a scenario in which you came to the location (i.e., the mall) to get the shoes. The 2023 commercial featured a much more individualized approach involving the story of one ordinary individual (not an actor), sharing in many real-life activities (obviously basketball but also flashbacks to childhood memories and time with parents), seeking to move "beyond" by overcoming the challenges in her life.

What do these comparisons tell us? The comparisons highlight potential clues in the culture to pay attention to, such as a more individualized approach in which growth and overcoming challenge matter to fulfill one's purpose based on one's gifts and interests. No longer are people as driven to connect in larger groups to simply do what the star does. People want to live their own stories based on who they are in authentic ways.

In my opinion, few mediums provide better opportunities for cultural analysis seeking interpretive clues than commercials. They offer direct insight into what is meaningful and relevant to people in their lives based on exhaustive research by marketers.

So what happens when we hold these three distinct disciplines—history, cognitive psychology, and marketing—in tension with one another, and then with discipleship in the local church? What common themes are found in all three disciplines? What overlaps can be noticed? What imaginative possibilities spring to mind when considering discipleship? What interpretations can we begin to make? What "how might we" questions rise up? What possibilities might emerge? These types of questions lead to potential interpretations around which to experiment our way forward in the realm of discipleship for today.

Following are some interpretive suggestions for discipleship based on the observation work already done around discipleship as well as interpretive possibilities stimulated by holding the noted disciplines in tension with one another.

INTERPRETATION: INSIGHTS FOR CROSSING THE DISCIPLESHIP CHASM TODAY

Interpretation: Focus on Multidimensional Solutions (Over One-Dimensional). How might a multidimensional approach be applied to discipleship in local congregations?

To reclaim a culture of faithful discipleship and experience something beautiful, today's local church must move beyond technical fixes and address the discipleship issue from multiple angles. Frameworks such as the Ephesians 4:11 model of apostles, prophets, evangelists, shepherds, and teachers, along with a focus on formational and generative approaches, allow for multifaceted discipleship applications.

In the local church setting in which I serve, we have found the language of being a "gathered" church to be helpful in describing a church focus that tends to be strong in the formative elements. The gathered community refers to what I would define as the "attractional-traditional-organized-inherited-institutional-established" form of church. Gathered church discipleship tends to involve what many Christians in America think of when they think of "church," including the average Sunday morning worship experience along with most established ministries in such a church setting. In general, the gathered church has traditionally been strong in formative teaching when it comes to discipleship.

Conversely, we have found that a church that has a strong focus on the generative elements that have been noted may be called a "sent" form of church. The sent community refers to what I would describe as a "pioneering-organic-incarnational-fresh-expression" approach to ministry. This mode of discipleship is directed primarily toward those with no knowledge of or experience in or life in the inherited church. The sent church tends to excel in new practices leading to generative realities. It involves meeting people on their turf in experimental ways to develop incarnational, authentic relationships, eventually leading to some form of worship.

Whereas the emphasis for the gathered community is to grow disciples by attracting people to join them by coming to their gathered space, the primary emphasis for the sent community is to make disciples by joining them in their space: by "going." To be clear, one mode of church is not to be considered superior to the other. Both bring strengths, with the gathered church offering a strong formational component and the sent church offering a strong generative component. *The idea is to understand how both, when held in proper tension in the same local church community, can yield new possibilities for reclaiming a multiplying discipleship.*

When my wife, Jenn, and I got married, we decided to take a cruise. On that cruise they offered dance lessons. We decided to take the lessons. What we quickly discovered was that dancing required a right tension between both partners whereby there was enough flexibility and trust to allow for improvisation, but enough structure to provide knowledge and direction for a particular type of dance. Unfortunately the only tension that Jenn and I experienced in those dancing lessons was the emotional kind of tension whereby we grew increasingly frustrated—and tense—with each other (to be fair and transparent, Jenn was actually a far better dancer than I!).

While Jenn and I did not experience a lot of dancing success as a result of those lessons, what they did teach me was the value of having a right tension. One of the keys to good dancing is to maintain proper tension between the partners. Too much tension results in a static, structured routine with little flair, imagination, or flexibility. Too little tension results in chaos, a lack of precision, an absence of direction, and partners who have no idea what the other one is doing.

But when the tension in the dance is just right, a beauty greater than what each individual partner could produce ensues. There is an exquisite ebb and flow between routine and creation and choreography and spontaneity. That flow then leads to inter-pretation for the next right steps (quite literally in the dancing world!).

IT IS POSSIBLE TO NAVIGATE THE HOLY TENSION BETWEEN FOCUSED STRUCTURE AND IMAGINATIVE RESPONSE.

The early church movement and the Wesleyan movement demonstrate it is possible to navigate the holy tension between fo-cused structure and imaginative response—resulting in a beauti-ful dance of flourishing, multiplying discipleship. The contexts of these movements were very different, but individuals in the early church and then in the Enlightenment period of the Wesleyan movement learned to dance in the context in which they found themselves. They learned to make informed interpretations that resulted in faithful discipleship movements. Whereas the early church navigated the dance during a time when tradition (think Pharisees) was incredibly important, Wesley learned to dance in a time when reason (think Hume and Kant) was paramount. What does such a dance look like in an age when it could be argued that experience often takes precedence over scripture?

As statistics reveal, many local churches have been unable to navigate the dance between the known and the unknown or between structured and improvised to foster healthy discipleship cultures. In these situations, pastors and congregations in gathered settings must begin to ask themselves if they trust each other enough to dance in a right tension and improvise as needed while exploring sent practices. Pastors and congregations must once again take a careful look at the challenges they are facing, examine the tensions that are before them, and make interpretations about what will help them move forward into deeper discipleship.

THREE INTERPRETIVE KEYS FOR CROSSING THE DISCIPLESHIP CHASM

Focus on the Generative Initiative Found in the Sent Community

Many churches today operate out of a heavily "shepherd-teacher" model. In this approach there are various benefits, particularly around fostering the strengths of a gathered church focus. However, this is not the primary model we see exemplified in the book of Acts. The early church was forced to adapt, explore, pioneer, and improvise as needed in order to connect with the wider culture in a relevant way.

Perhaps this was why the apostle Paul once stated, "To the weak I became weak, to win the weak. I have become all things to all people so that by all possible means I might save some. I do all this for the sake of the gospel, that I may share in its blessings" (1 Corinthians 9:22-23 NIV).

In other words, Paul improvised as needed in order to connect with new people where they were in order to foster new life.

Today's local churches must again discover the passion of living on the fringes of society and letting that passion drive them to try new things. So many local churches today have very little apostolic initiative. Because John Wesley felt compelled to share the gospel with everyone and to spread scriptural holiness over the land, he had, out of necessity, a willingness to experiment, risk, fail, and deal with opposition. The result was a fresh approach to ministry in his context.

One other result of Wesley's improvisation to reach the masses included a liberation of the laity for leadership. Wesley knew he could not reach everyone. Thus he knew he had to empower and equip others to lead, serve as spiritual guides, and perform priestly roles. What might such an apostolic impulse mean for today's local churches?

A number of years ago we realized in our local church setting that ministry efforts that had always previously worked no longer did to the same degree. Despite seeking to offer increased excellence in preaching, youth programs, pastoral care, children's ministry, and high-quality music, we noticed that there was increasingly less return on investment. Fewer new people were coming. Growth was not as fast as we were accustomed to. Ministry vitality was ever more difficult to maintain. Eventually we learned we were not alone as the culture around us transitioned toward an increasingly less church-centric reality.

Despite the fact that we were not alone in this reality, I personally found my own anxiety rising. As the lead pastor I felt the pressure to have the right answer to our increased ministry struggles. More and more I applied every technical solution I could envision—ever better preaching techniques, better discipleship programs, stronger life groups, hiring better staff, more teaching with staff, more effective communication methods, a new governance structure, etc. Still our ministry vitality was not improving at the rate I had hoped. I increasingly did not know what to do.

It was at this time that something very unexpected occurred. At the time, my good friend Kris was a seminary student. He was taking a church-planting class and asked if he could use our church as a case study for some of his work. I did not think we had anything to lose, so I said yes to the invitation. After spending many weeks observing our church culture, practices, and procedures, the student asked an interpretive question that would eventually lead to a series of experiments and interventions in the life of our church that we never expected. The question that was raised was, *Rather than seeking to gather a thousand people in one location [which would be difficult anywhere, but especially in central Pennsylvania], how might we consider reaching a thousand people in a hundred gatherings of ten people each?*

This was a question that would ultimately push us to embrace a much more sent mindset and generative impulse. This was an interpretive question that would have many implications for future interventions in our church. It was a question that would force us to consider who we were as well as who we would become.

Reclaim the Power Found in a Focus on Proper Formation in the Gathered Community

---

Historically, the power of the gathered community through the offices of teaching and shepherding and prophesying was to offer formation in Christ in word and deed. But many local churches today have turned the *formational* journey into an *informational* process. This was not the original intent of shepherding, prophesying, and teaching. As local churches have failed to live into formational habits of the faith, the vitality of many churches has correspondingly declined in direct proportion with the lack of discipleship. The result, then, is a flawed understanding in which clergy have often come to resemble social workers, counselors, and CEOs, rather than preachers fostering and equipping the offices of apostles, prophets, evangelists, shepherds, and teachers.

The purpose of gathering was never for remaining "simply gathered." Rather, the purpose of gathering was to experience the tension of a formation that led to generation. This tension was employed in the early catechesis of the church as individuals emphasized a discipleship dominated by right thinking in the Kingdom, which led to right living in the Kingdom.

Said more succinctly, proper gathering leads to proper sending.

Embrace Both/And over Either/Or

Many churches choose to operate in an either/or mode and thus are not experiencing multiplying discipleship. They exist as an attractional, institutional church focused strictly on gathering for themselves, or they operate only to connect with new people in a sent mode but then often fail to develop a deep habitus of formational discipleship through learning and growth. Many churches are threatened by a dual-expression approach. Making disciples falls into a completely different category than outreach. Hospitality is viewed entirely separately from mission. Yet, must this be so? Is it possible for radical hospitality to result in a missional imperative? Or for reaching out to be a first step in making disciples? Might holding in tension elements that are often isolated yield new possibilities?

When today's local church can learn to reclaim the holy tension displayed by the early church, a faithful discipleship may again be found. The spread of the Christian faith in both the early church and the Wesleyan movement occurred in part because of a multiplying discipleship in which deep beliefs directly informed faithful practices. The discipleship tension served as a catalyst forward, even in non-Christian environments, in authentic and relevant ways.

Part of the genius of Wesley was that he was simultaneously intentional (a more gathered-community trait) and flexible (a more sent-community trait). Wesley sought to implement plans but also to adjust and improvise as needed as life occurred. This both/and approach is exactly what today's local church must embrace in an ever-changing world.

What might it look like if every local church learned to embrace a both/and tension, in the gifts of both the gathered and sent communities, so that the offices of apostles, prophets, evangelists, shepherds, and teachers could again be lived out to the fullest degree? Such a both/and approach could very well serve as the catalyst for a healthy culture of multiplying discipleship, no matter the context in which the discipleship was being lived out.

In our setting one of the images that has proven helpful to consider in embracing a both/and approach has been the image of a double helix. Imagine that one strand of the double helix holds the attributes of the gathered community, with a focus on shepherding, teaching, and prophesying. Gifts that the gathered side can offer include elements such as stability, resources for organized discipleship opportunities, being visible in the community, and a centralized organization.

Imagine the other strand of the double helix holding descriptors of the sent community, with a focus on apostleship and evangelism. Gifts of the sent side of discipleship include nimbleness, an evangelistic orientation, pioneering in entrepreneurial ways, existing in the community, and operating in a more decentralized manner. Now imagine these gathered and sent gifts being held together in an endless, healthy, ebbing and flowing tension—influencing one another, through Jesus. These concepts can be summarized in this way:

GATHERED (S-P-T)		SENT (A-E)
Stable	J	Nimble
Discipleship Oriented	E	Evangelistically Oriented
Resourced	S	Entrepreneurial
Established	U	Organic
Centralized	S	Decentralized

This framework provides a helpful, interpretive lens through which to view any activity in the church to bring about a sharper discipleship focus. Such an interpretive framework fosters helpful discipleship questions around any activity connected to the life of the church.

For example:

- How might we take our gathered student ministry and infuse more sent DNA into it? What might such a tension yield?

- How might we take an outreach effort, such as a food pantry, and infuse more gathered DNA into it? What might such a tension yield?

- How might we take a gathered resource, such as a church facility, and use it in a more sent manner? What might such a tension yield?

- How might we take an organic gathering, such as a rugby group, and incorporate more gathered elements? What might such a tension yield?

Such tension-filled questions can be asked around every current church activity or resource to yield interpretive possibilities when it comes to discipleship.

In a more general manner the questions become: How can our gathered side inform our sent side? And how can our sent side inform our gathered side?

These questions can be asked at a corporate level, but also at an individual level. When we ask such interpretive questions, it starts to become clear where growth in discipleship is needed. Do we need to grow in more formational ways, as the gathered focus lends itself toward, or do we need to grow in more generative ways, as the sent focus lends itself toward?

In this way, these types of interpretive questions can begin to offer both new possibilities and forms of accountability. When asked on a regular basis, these interpretive questions serve as correctives to drifting too much into "only formational" or "only generative" practices. For example, if some need to grow into deeper generative practices in their discipleship, the day will come when they are doing that and actually need to return to a greater focus on formational learning. Conversely individuals who need to grow in deeper formational teaching will need to increase their generative practices after they have sought to grow in formative practices for an extended season.

In these ways, formation and generation feed seamlessly off each other. Proper formation leads to proper generation. Proper hospitality leads to mission. Proper sharing of the good news leads to proper learning of the good news. It is a holy tension involving multiple focal points resulting in a much more powerful form of discipleship.

Today's followers of Jesus Christ again have the opportunity to interpret their way into uncharted territories through a renewed focus on discipleship that is both formative and generative in nature. The fullness of life in Christ is realized not just in the teachings of Jesus but also in the practices and applications of Jesus Himself. Behavior must match knowledge. The road is both known, through information believed, and traveled, through actions taken. In this way, a thriving new life of depth and spiritual health may burst forth through a reclaimed pathway of healthy discipleship.

BEHAVIOR MUST MATCH KNOWLEDGE.

What we are discovering is that in this rapidly changing world, when it comes to discipleship, observation leads to helpful interpretation. And helpful interpretation leads to relevant steps of discipleship intervention.

It is to those discipleship steps—intervention—that we now turn.

INTERPRETATION QUESTIONS FOR CROSSING
THE DISCIPLESHIP CHASM

1. As a general formula, take some of the observations you have noted and begin to ask "How might we" questions related to them.

   • For example, "We have observed that most of our discipleship focus is within the walls of our facility. How might we give greater focus to sending disciples beyond our walls?"

- Or: "We have observed that we offer occasional discipleship learning opportunities. How might we offer a more continuous discipleship focus?"

- Or: "We have observed almost all of our discipleship emphasis prioritizes formation. How might we give more intentionality to generation?"

2. Take some time to view some popular advertisements being shared in the wider culture. What themes or trends are being lifted up? How are advertisements seeking to be relevant to their audiences? What lessons might be discovered and applied when it comes to discipleship in the church?

3. What clues do the early church and Wesleyan movements have for churches today in relation to discipleship?

4. How might proper formation in the faith lead to more generation?

5. How might a framework such as the offices of apostles, prophets, evangelists, shepherds, and teachers be incorporated into the life of your church?

6. How might the tension between formation and generation be a gift rather than a barrier?

7. Filter every discipleship activity in your setting through the Gathered/Sent matrix. How might each discipleship activity be influenced by the opposite side of the matrix in which it falls? How might the tension of a gathered and sent approach yield new possibilities for discipleship? For example:

8. How might a Bible study happening on Wednesday nights at the church (a gathered discipleship activity) be influenced or altered by applying some sent characteristics to it?

9. How might a gathering among friends every week at the gym (a more sent discipleship opportunity) be influenced or altered by applying some gathered characteristics to it?

10. How might we take a gathered children's ministry and infuse more sent DNA into it? What might such a tension yield?

11. What outreach efforts do we currently have going on? How can we infuse more gathered DNA into them? What might such a tension yield?

12. How might we view more gathered resources through a distinctly sent set of lenses? What might such a tension yield?

13. Taking note of our more informal gatherings already occurring, how might we incorporate more gathered elements in those places in an intentional way? What might such a tension yield?

14. How might we take a hiking group and infuse more gathered elements into it?

15. How might we take mentoring relationships and introduce more formal teaching into them?

Chapter Three

INTERVENTION: EMBRACING DISCIPLESHIP TENSION TO CROSS THE DISCIPLESHIP CHASM

Let's get more practical.

As my friend J. R. once said to me: *"Men and women: we don't have a leadership problem in the church. We don't have a money problem in the church. We don't have a participation problem in the church. We have a discipleship problem in the church."*

Or as my doctoral mentor shared, *"Discipleship is not assenting to a belief system, operating out of some political norms, or subscribing to a political agenda. Discipleship is recognizing, receiving, releasing, and reproducing Jesus."*

They are so right!

But of course the big question becomes how. How do we address the discipleship problems before us?

The concept of discipleship is nothing new. The issue of discipleship has been around as long as Jesus Himself when He began journeying with the original twelve disciples. And yet many local congregations are not sure how to actually engage with those in their midst in meaningful discipleship.

When it comes to the topic of discipleship, many churches seem to choose one extreme approach of discipleship or another. Many churches have such a loose system of discipleship that there really is no intentionality of discipleship at all. They may have strong relational components, but these relations are often based on a fellowship devoid of formative intentionality. These churches have no discipleship pathway, no entry point to be discipled, no metrics to determine if discipleship is occurring, and no resources given specifically for discipleship purposes. The result—unsurprisingly—is a lack of intentional spiritual formation.

Other churches have a very rigid, programmatic, yet often sterile approach to discipleship. There may be a clearly defined discipleship pathway, but it is often little more than helping individuals join as official members of a congregation while perhaps taking a few spiritual gift inventories along the way. The focus tends to be on information offered rather than a shared, experiential, formational discipleship opportunity. Oftentimes the heavily programmatic approaches to discipleship involve excessive content provided but little focus on practice or mentorship. Thus the result more often than not is the raising up of competent, institutional church volunteers, but not disciples.

The result of either of these one-dimensional approaches is essentially the same—a lack of genuine discipleship. While these one-dimensional approaches may be easier to execute due to a lack of the tension or complexity found in a both/and approach around formation and generation, the net result is a shallow—at best—form of discipleship. The reality is that most churches are not willing to engage in or are unaware of the possibility of engaging in the tension between informal discipleship practices and informational programs of content. Yet this is a tension needed if authentic, rugged discipleship is to be lived out in local churches.

THE DISCIPLESHIP RESULT FOR THE EFFORTS OF MOST CHURCHES IS THE RAISING UP OF COMPETENT, INSTITUTIONAL, CHURCH VOLUNTEERS— BUT NOT DISCIPLES OF JESUS.

The early church provides a model of living into this discipleship tension and offers clues for how we can best live into it today. To be very clear about what exactly we are trying to do—we must be precise on the what, why, and how of discipleship.

For many churches, the what and the why are generally understood. The "what" is to raise up disciples of Jesus Christ. For our purposes here we are defining a disciple as a follower of Jesus. More specifically, *we will define a disciple as someone who believes in Jesus while actively following Jesus, being transformed by Jesus, and remaining committed to the mission of Jesus (Matthew 4:19).* Notice the elements of practice and missional impulse present in this definition of discipleship along with the belief in Christ Himself.

There is also general agreement on the "why" of discipleship. The why comes directly from the mandate that Jesus Himself gives. At the very end of the Gospel of Matthew we hear Jesus give this command: "Therefore go and make disciples of all nations, baptizing them in the name of the Father and of the Son and of the Holy Spirit, and teaching them to obey everything I have commanded you. And surely I am with you always, to the very end of the age" (Matthew 28:19-20 NIV).

Jesus could not be any more clear or explicit in His expectation that followers of Christ "make disciples." It is particularly striking that these are the final words that Jesus gives at the very end of the Gospel of Matthew. Final words tend to carry more importance or at least more intentionality than most words. When someone retires or is about to say goodbye, they share only the most important message. There is no time for fluff or trivial matters. Only the essential message is shared. Here, for Jesus, the crucial message He wants to communicate is to make disciples. If this is the last thing that Jesus shares in this Gospel it is worth taking extra note of it. If Jesus commands discipleship (and He does), and Jesus communicates this in His final words (which He does), then those are compelling reasons for our why.

In this way discipleship is not an extra religious obligation to check off on our moral checklist. Nor is discipleship a program of religious activities to achieve. Discipleship is lived out of the deep love we have with Christ Himself. It is deeply personal. It is intimate. At the same time it is formative. And generative. It impacts individuals. It impacts communities of believers. And therefore it impacts the world. Healthy churches simply cannot exist, much less thrive, without a healthy culture of discipleship.

I have always loved how author Neil Cole proclaims this reality in such a blunt manner when he shares: "Ultimately each church will be evaluated by only one thing. It's disciples. Your church is only as good as its disciples. It does not matter how good your praise, preaching, programs, or property are. If your disciples are passive, needy, consumerist, and not moving in the direction of radical obedience, your church is not good."[1]

Those are some strong words! But they carry truth.

Thus, because Jesus mandates discipleship, and because discipleship is essential to the individual and corporate health of Jesus followers, we discover a most compelling "why" to discipleship.

Local churches that get the issue of discipleship right—or even partly right—are going to experience higher levels of vitality than those that do not focus on discipleship in healthy ways. The higher the level of commitment to and intentionality about healthy discipleship—through the tension of presenting formal

1. Neil Cole, *Ordinary Hero: Becoming a Disciple Who Makes a Difference* (Grand Rapids, MI: Baker Books, 2008), 185.

content and experiential practices—the higher the level of local church health that occurs.

What we discover then is that the primary issue around the lack of discipleship in most local churches is usually not an intentional resistance to its importance (the why) or a lack of understanding it (the what). Rather, the primary issue is increasingly around *how* to foster authentic discipleship in local churches.

For clues today on how to foster the tension between the formative and generative realities of discipleship being advocated in this book, we once again find the early church movement offers helpful clues that apply to us today.

INTERVENTION: COMPREHEND AND WALK THE WAY

I first remember learning about the Appian Way clear back in the seventh grade. This Roman road was officially known as the Via Appia. It was constructed in 312 BCE and covered 132 Roman miles. The road served as a major commercial route and allowed for robust trade with other parts of the world. It contributed greatly to Rome's influence in the known world at that time. The Appian Way was known for being a strategic commercial lifeline for the Roman Empire because of several important trade routes that converged along it.

In the ancient Roman Empire, roads were the only way to get from one place to another over land since airplanes (obviously!) did not yet exist. Because of this reality, roads became symbols of power, life, and destination as they were traveled. Then, as now, having the information that a road existed was important because one cannot travel a road if one does not know about it. Simultaneously, a road was only useful in getting to a destination and fostering vitality if the information about the road was combined with the practice of traveling it. The tension between right knowledge and right practice of the road was the key to navigating it well. Once again we see how the tension between knowing and doing produces a way forward. In this case, with the Appian Way, it was a literal way forward where there previously had been no way.

In this context, individuals could say they knew of the way, meaning they knew a certain road existed—whether they actually traveled it or not. With time, the term "the way" evolved to take on more meaning. It became more figurative and could describe not only knowledge about but also knowledge that informed practice. In the New Testament writings, the term "The Way" took on an even more specific meaning. Jesus even identified Himself as the Way leading to God the Father (John 14:6). Eventually, by the time the early church began to take root, followers of Jesus became known as followers of the Way (Acts 9:2; 19:9, 23).

Notice what this description of early Jesus disciples entails— that followers of Jesus were marked by a distinctive belief and practice that was informed by that belief. In this we see, again, the combination of both distinctive living (action) and beliefs (information). The tension of both generative and formative elements was a necessary reality for disciples of the Way to bring forth a healthy fruition of the Kingdom of God.

I love the connection between the Appian Way as a literal road to foster commercial vitality where there previously had not been such vitality, and Jesus as the Way to life and truth in God. In this way, disciples of Jesus become those who walk the way of God, with God, and to God in order to foster life and vitality in the Kingdom of God.

Understanding that the Way of Jesus involves both information and practice is crucial for both early followers of Jesus and disciples today. Just as one never reaches the exciting destination of a road without actually traveling on it, so followers of Christ never reach the fullness of the Way without living into the tension of putting into practice the knowledge they possess. When churches choose to live outside of this tension (focusing on all belief but no action, or lots of action without defined truth), deep discipleship will not occur. This refusal or inability to live into this tension would seem to be a key reason why many of today's churches are experiencing rapid decline. Correspondingly, the embracing of this tension between belief and action is also why there have been times when the Christian movement has flourished (as was previously noted regarding the early church and Wesleyan movements).

While local churches and discipleship pathway curricula should be commended for imparting information and knowledge of Christ, many are missing resulting practices to live into that knowledge of Christ. In these instances, without the tension that comes with accompanying practices, the likelihood of faith generation is minimal.

I was fascinated to learn years ago that in the early church, the baptismal process usually involved three years. The goal in this time frame was not simply to impart teachings about the faith; the goal also included application of the faith through apprenticeship and mentoring. In this way, the focus was not just on doctrine or on practice but on both.

Only as individuals were steeped in discipleship with right knowledge and right practice would they be equipped to live countercultural lives even in the face of persecution. These early

Christians were able to offer a witness to the world through their actions, which had been intentionally formed in the faith. This witnessing then led, over time, to new life in new converts in the faith. In this way the formation led to actions that resulted in generation. In short, the combination of information and practice resulted in an experience of generative, multiplying discipleship.

Perhaps this is why the famous early Christian writer and apologist Tertullian once famously said, "Christians are made, not born."[2]

Part of the power in living out the tension between information and practice is that it results in what could be termed an "embodied knowledge." Embodied knowledge involves knowledge that informs action through careful study and application of the faith. In this way, individuals are not simply kind or caring or loving or sacrificial just to be "good" people. Rather, disciples of Christ seek to embody the way of their master, Jesus. Rabbis in the time period when Jesus lived had students who would literally walk in the footsteps of their rabbi as part of their learning. The learning influenced how they lived. Disciples of Jesus seek to do the same today. They walk, model, and practice the faith as a result of proper formation in the ways of Christ Himself.

Today we tend to pass out books or materials from approved programs to share content of the faith and hope this results in mature discipleship. As we are increasingly discovering, it rarely does. Content alone is rarely sufficient to foster lives of transformed embodiment in Christ. In the early church, one of the earliest "Christian training manuals" was the Didache.[3] Potential mem-

---

2. Tertullian, *Apology: De Spectaculis*, trans. T. R. Glover (Cambridge, MA: Harvard University Press, 1931), 177.

3. Thomas O'Loughlin, *The Didache: A Window on the Earliest Christians* (Grand Rapids, MI: Baker Academic, 2010), 35.

bers learned what the text of the Didache meant in the life of the faith community of which they were a part. Individuals learned in apprenticeship with more mature community members who were farther along in their faith journeys.

Examining these actions held in tension in the early church provides clues for interventions in forming vibrant discipleship cultures today. As has been noted, combined formational and generative practices such as ongoing mentoring, missional discipleship, connecting with nonbelievers, a more extended catechesis, embracing the priesthood of all believers, testimony sharing, radical hospitality and generosity, community engagement, planting of new faith communities, sacrificial living, contextual living, extended prayer, the learning of doctrine, a focus on truth, and faith formation—simultaneously existing in tension—are almost always absent from any discipleship pathway or congregational alignment in local churches.

Also absent from discipleship journeys are tensions held in any framework that seeks to hold together formative and generative realities. This is why frameworks such as the previously mentioned APEST list (Apostles, Prophets, Evangelists, Shepherds, Teachers), found in Ephesians 4:11 and advocated by author Alan Hirsh, are so helpful today. This APEST model is one that embraces both knowledge and practice.

DISCIPLESHIP FRAMEWORKS THAT FOCUS ON INFORMATION AND EXPEDIENCY, WHILE LACKING FORMATION AND PATIENCE, PRODUCE CONSUMERS RATHER THAN CHRISTIANS.

Discipleship frameworks that focus on expediency or information and lack formation produce consumeristic Christians. Consumeristic Christians enjoy consuming teaching, learning, and information but rarely put the learning into practice. Because there is extensive taking in of information, and little living out, individuals then become spiritually obese. Conversely, discipleship frameworks that focus only on action and practice, without taking time to dwell on truth and doctrine, run the risk of spiritual malnourishment.

The early Christian movement was able to walk the fine line between spiritual obesity and spiritual malnutrition, resulting in lifestyles that embodied the knowledge learned. In this way the early Christian movement points us to particular interactions that today's churches can model for healthy discipleship.

INTERVENTION: EMBRACING THE TENSION OF FORMAL AND INFORMAL TODAY

Elements of Formal Discipleship

Many churches do formational discipleship marked by formal practices very well and have already implemented elements of formal discipleship in the life of the church. Such elements might include prepared Bible studies led by a staff person or equipped volunteer, planned worship services led by a pastor, preplanned mission trips, organized outreach and service opportunities, and daily devotional plans. These more formational elements have benefitted many in their discipleship journeys.

Once more, formal discipleship is important. We see formal discipleship modeled by Jesus. When Jesus offers his first sermon at the synagogue and opens the scrolls to reference the prophet Isaiah (Luke 4:16–17), when Jesus teaches and preaches the Sermon on the Mount with large crowds gathered (Matthew 5:1–2), and when Jesus teaches to large crowds from a boat (Mark 4:1), we see Jesus offering forms of formal discipleship.

Formal discipleship is helpful for formation in strengthening beliefs and providing clarity around doctrine. However, as noted, if a church focuses only on formal discipleship, the likelihood of a robust discipleship is minimal. While Jesus demonstrated formal discipleship, he also modeled another side of discipleship that could be labeled informal discipleship.

Elements of Informal Discipleship

Jesus spent significant time teaching his disciples. But nowhere in scripture do we ever see or hear Jesus instructing His disciples to take out their pencils and tablets in order to correctly answer all of the formalized test questions that Jesus was about to ask. Instead, Jesus often taught and formed His disciples through more informal means of discipleship that involved practices embodying the faith in word and deed.

Informal discipleship includes practices such as eating together, mentoring, asking questions, experimenting, interacting with those outside of the faith, exploring new spaces and opportunities, empowering, sharing life together, and living into common experiences. One could easily argue that Jesus spent more time focused on informal discipleship with disciples than He did with formal discipleship.

Any time the disciples of Jesus ask Him to explain a parable, any time Jesus and His disciples walk to a next town, any time Jesus sends His disciples out to heal, any time Jesus prays with His disciples, any time Jesus models compassion and mercy to the least and the lost, any time He serves with His disciples, any time they have conversation, any time the disciples eat together—these are all instances of informal discipleship. In fact, the Gospel of John spends five whole chapters (John 13–17) describing for us one powerful, extended, informal discipleship encounter as Jesus prays for His disciples, washes their feet, shares in the institution of the Last Supper, teaches, and offers His final words to them before His impending death.

Whereas formal discipleship tends to focus more on orthodoxy, informal discipleship focuses more on orthopraxy. Whereas formal discipleship tends to be more organized in nature, informal discipleship is more decentralized. Whereas formal discipleship is more structured, informal discipleship is more messy. The point here is not that one is better than another. *The point is that a right tension between both realities of formal and informal discipleship is needed in order to adequately rediscover authentic discipleship for the day and age in which we live.*

Intervening around Tension

Informal discipleship is powerful and needed because it involves the application of discipleship practices in real life. However, informal discipleship requires great intentionality on the part of those who would seek to do life together. If they are not careful, a focus exclusively on informal discipleship can lead to a lack of intentionality that becomes haphazard in the formation of discipleship. Some churches only live into informal discipleship without any formal discipleship pathway. The risk for these churches is that there is no corporate approach to fostering discipleship. Discipleship becomes driven primarily by individuals, at an individual level, which can exclude the needs and recognition of a corporate understanding. In other words, informal discipleship gives greater focus to orthopraxy, but can do so at the expense of orthodoxy.

While a tension between both formal and informal discipleship realities is needed for a robust discipleship, most of today's local congregations are not engaged in living into such a tension. Local churches today are either unaware that such a tension is needed, unwilling to seek to embrace the tension, or unsure of how to live in such a tension. No wonder multiplying discipleship is so difficult to discover in so many churches. Yet when it is discovered, there is new life to be found, not only for those practicing the faith but also for those outside the faith, in relevant, meaningful, and powerful ways.

During my doctoral program at Portland Seminary I had the distinct privilege of learning with and from Dr. Len Sweet. This was such a blessing in my life and a time I will always treasure. One day Len shared a story that has stayed with me and at the same time has provided for me and for my church a model of how to live into the tension of formative and generative discipleship. His experience demonstrated to me what can happen when formal and informal practices can be engaged—in any context—in such a way that multiplying discipleship might be cultivated.

Len shared that many years ago he was working in England and that his daughter had joined him on the trip. Len promised his daughter they would take at least a day to go and do whatever his daughter wanted while they were in England. When that day came (it was a Wednesday), Len's daughter chose to go to Westminster Abbey. However, when they arrived, there was a wait out the door and it cost 15 pounds (the equivalent of 20 American dollars). Len did not have the inclination to either wait in line or pay to get into a church. So Len and his daughter left and decided to come back the following Sunday morning during the actual worship hour.

When they arrived for the worship service they discovered neither a wait to get in nor any amount they had to pay. Once inside the large space, they discovered only about 150 people in attendance. About 50 of the folks there were in the choir. Another 50 were visitors, and once they discovered it was a real worship service they left. That left only about 50 participants for worship.

After letting us, as the students, listen and observe this story with him, Len began asking some interpretive questions: "Why was this the case? Why will people pay and wait in line during the week for a tour of Westminster Abbey, but not actually come for an authentic worship experience where you do not have to pay?" Then Len began to offer a few interpretations. Len noted how what people pay for on a normal tour is a tour guide who will walk with them step by step and make the history of that place relevant to the guest. So what were people paying for? They were paying for the authentic experience of someone walking with them step by step and sharing the history and story of Westminster Abbey in a way to which they could relate.

Look what Len was offering in his interpretation—engagement through formal and informal means. In this story we see an informal focus with the guide who walks personally step by step with people for them to have a meaningful experience. We also see a formal component in the sharing of the historical information and facts about Westminster Abbey. Both are needed in tension with each other to fully experience and appreciate Westminster Abbey.

What might such a model mean or look like for today's local churches when it comes to the issue of discipleship? What steps can be taken, both formal and informal, held in tension with one another? This model means finding ways to remember, celebrate, and lift up doctrine and the history of faith. Perhaps this means giving increased intentionality to formal practices in the life of the congregation. *Where there is no discipleship there will be no thriving as a congregation.* It is that simple. Thus the starting point toward healthy discipleship for any church is to commit with intentionality toward discipleship. To be clear, commitment to discipleship means more than a few individuals taking their discipleship journeys more seriously. Commitment to discipleship means a congregation-wide intentionality and alignment. So if there are not formal means by which the truth and doctrines and history of the church are shared in a local congregation, such means must be developed and instituted. Perhaps this means forming congregational alignment around discipleship, setting up times for learning more about the faith, engaging in spiritual inventories, or more Bible study time.

A CULTURE OF DISCIPLESHIP WILL INVOLVE A CONGREGATION-WIDE INTENTIONALITY AND ALIGNMENT AROUND DISCIPLESHIP.

At the same time, these formal opportunities must be accompanied by more informal means by which the faith is shared and fostered through authentic discipleship practices in a more personal, step-by-step manner—for however long it might take. Perhaps this means fostering more mentoring opportunities, one-on-one conversations, personal invitations, organic exploration of discipleship over time, activation of each person's unique gifts, a commitment to empowering people in new directions, and fostering individuals' calls rather than filling corporate volunteer slots.

What might such interventions look like at a practical level?

Years ago, for a variety of reasons, our local congregation made a radical shift in how it approached discipleship. I would like to say that I, in my great wisdom, encouraged this change. However, this would be far from the truth. The reality was that God, in God's grace, allowed circumstances to push us to places we would have never gone on our own.

The result was a new, tension-filled (in the best way!) approach to engaging discipleship that sought to be both structured and flexible . . . intentional and organic . . . formal and informal . . . focused on orthodoxy and focused on orthopraxy . . . in short—formative and generative discipleship. Many churches have some form of programmatic discipleship path. We created an experience that we have entitled Disciple's Journey. It involves a continual invitation into four individual steps based on a tension between connection, discovery, engagement, and multiplication. This journey provides a consistent intentionality but also leaves space for messiness and organic timing.

Following is a general overview of what these steps of discipleship intervention have looked like in our local church setting. You do not need to directly replicate this model, although you may. But look for the elements, ideas, and clues that are transferrable to your context.

INTERVENTION: CROSSING THE DISCIPLESHIP CHASM
DISCIPLE'S JOURNEY STEP 1

The first two steps of this Disciple's Journey may outwardly look similar to steps that many churches take (although the orientation in steps 1 and 2 of Disciple's Journey is different). Our step 1 is focused on connection. People connect with God and our church through the completion of five informational sessions. This step involves a lot of content being shared about the DNA and vision of the church, a connection with some of our staff, opportunities to get involved, and a chance for dialogue where questions can be answered. At the end of this step focused on connection, people can join in the life of the church through formal discipleship if they so wish. We do not make it overly difficult to join in the life of the church. Our goal is to help people to connect and then help them grow deeper in discipleship and faith.

DISCIPLE'S JOURNEY STEP 2

The second step of this Disciple's Journey involves six informational sessions focused on people discovering their gifts and passions through strengths assessments, spiritual gift inventories, and surveys. Many churches also have a step somewhat similar to this. In this case, however, individuals are not raised up with the goal of becoming church volunteers. They are specifically introduced to the concept of exploring discipleship tensions and how those tensions will form their life of discipleship.

DISCIPLE'S JOURNEY STEP 3

In step 3, through eight generative sessions (although the number of sessions does fluctuate depending on how many people are participating), a shift occurs from a "content-first" approach to a "practice-first" approach in which individuals put into practice what they have been learning. Practices such as the sharing of one's faith, prayer, offering testimony, committing to new areas of service and leadership, and navigating discipleship tensions are all employed. This is the stage that many churches do not offer with any intentionality—but it's a place where we have seen great growth and new life emerge. We have seen, repeatedly, the embracing of discipleship tensions lead to new life through practices previously not employed.

Notice in this step the mention of "discipleship tensions." Of particular importance in step 3 (and introduced at the end of step 2) is a full focus on discipleship tensions that are cross-referenced with each individual's gifts and passions. The exploration of these tensions provides a way for individuals (and churches) to assess where they currently are in their discipleship journey as well as where they need to grow. This exploration requires a sense of openness, vulnerability, self-disclosure, interpretation, and messiness. To combat a bit of the messiness, a few more formal means are utilized. Individuals are asked to provide a ranking on a scale of 1 to 10—but avoiding a 5—for each discipleship tension (described below), noting where they currently see themselves in their discipleship. The goal is to help individuals discover which side of four discipleship continuums they find themselves on. By doing so, individuals can hold in tension an awareness of how they are naturally gifted to grow in discipleship and what discipleship areas they may still need to grow toward. The particular discipleship continuums that individuals and churches are invited to explore are the tensions of Formal-Informal, Deep-New, Belief-Behavior, Gathered-Sent.

The definitions of these tensions are as follows.

Formal-Informal

In formal discipleship settings, disciples grow through organized opportunities occurring on a regular or scheduled basis. These opportunities are often very programmatic in nature. Practices such as organized Bible studies, regular Sunday morning worship, regularly planned financial giving amounts, and weekly life groups would fall under this category. When Jesus taught at synagogues (Mark 1:21; Luke 13:10) and preached the sermon on the Mount (Matthew 5–7), He was modeling a more formal type of discipleship.

In informal discipleship settings, disciples grow through incarnational interactions that seek to help people become more Christlike through organic practices and relationships as they arise. In life there may be no better example of informal discipleship than parenting. Parents seek to guide, encourage, celebrate, and discipline their kids through everyday life. Investing in spiritual friendships can be another informal discipleship practice. In this instance the growth in discipleship is stimulated by conversation, modeling, listening, and asking questions in more organic life situations. Yet another practice that falls in the category of informal discipleship is mentoring. Mentoring involves conversation as well, but also modeling as the mentor demonstrates what the follower should do. When Jesus answered the questions of His disciples (Matthew 17:19), engaged in conversation while walking from one location to another (Mark 8:2), or modeled for the disciples particular practices (such as washing one another's feet in John 13 or sharing in the Last Supper in Matthew 26), He was sharing in informal discipleship with His disciples. Finally, choosing to give generously and spontaneously to meet observed, organic needs as they arise would be another informal discipleship practice.

A key question to ask in this tension to determine where one is on the scale of 1 (most formal) to 10 (most informal) would be:

Would discipleship be more effective if it became more intentionally structured or if it became more available/responsive in organic ways? If someone felt they were already growing in a more formal discipleship manner but needed to grow in an informal manner, they would answer in the 1–4 range. If someone felt they were already growing in a more informal discipleship manner but needed to grow in a more formal discipleship manner, they would answer in the 6–10 range.

Deep-New

In deep discipleship opportunities, existing disciples are growing by focusing on going deep in their faith. Formal opportunities that can focus on going deeper in faith would include learning through Bible study, reading, listening to teachings, focusing on sermons, strengthening one's beliefs, and utilizing a trained spiritual coach. These discipleship opportunities would focus more heavily on the shepherding and teaching offices of APEST.

Some informal practices that would help individuals go deep in their faith might include journaling (where one reflects on circumstances, passions, and hopes to see where and how God is at work in one's life), engaging in spiritual conversations with a friend in a coffee shop, and taking a long walk or hike in nature with no technology in order to simply commune with God.

In new discipleship opportunities, the focus of discipleship is on growing by reaching new people in the faith. Here the goal is the spreading of faith with individuals who have no faith connection. Some formal opportunities that focus on sharing the faith could involve supporting missionaries, attending organized mission trips, creating radical hospitality, organizing prayer vigils for God's spirit to open the hearts of those closed off to God, and "bring a friend to worship" Sundays when individuals are encouraged to bring friends who might not know Jesus. Organized revival events could also be a formal opportunity to focus on new discipleship.

Examples of informal discipleship possibilities focused on fostering new life in others in the faith include trying new endeavors to reach new believers on their turf, such as a dinner church experience (often outside of identified church facilities), having spiritual conversations with nonbelievers, and taking prayer walks in the community to discover pain points to address with people in relevant ways. These discipleship opportunities would focus more heavily on the apostle and evangelist offices of APEST.

A key question to ask in this tension continuum to determine where one is on the scale of 1 (deep) to 10 (new) would be: *Would discipleship be more effective if it focused on strengthening existing believers in Christ or if it focused on reaching new believers in Christ?* If someone felt they were already going deeper in their faith but not reaching others with the good news of Christ, they would be in the 1–4 range. If someone felt they were connecting well with new people in the faith but were not doing much to strengthen the belief they already had, they would answer in the 6–10 range.

Belief-Behavior

In discipleship settings focused on belief, disciples seek to transform the mind by imparting knowledge and engaging with scripture. Discipleship focused in this direction values learning and informational input to help strengthen one's belief. Activities that focus on an exploration of theology and content consumption (such as Bible study, reading, and podcasts) fall in this category.

The reality in our current, Western church culture is that most discipleship efforts default to belief over behavior.

In discipleship settings focused on behavior, disciples grow through taking action that seeks to equip a person to become more Christlike through what they do. This focus involves a more external reality where the actions can be seen. Practices such as serving in an area of need, praying over someone who needs it, giving (both in time and finances), connecting with nonbelievers, and offering entrepreneurial leadership would fall under this discipleship category. Disciples who focus on their behaviors act differently (in a way that can be observed by others) than non-believers. In most churches, it is this behavioral component of discipleship that is lacking.

A key question to ask in this tension to determine where one is on the scale of 1 (belief) to 10 (behavior) would be: *Would discipleship be more effective if it focused on what a person needs to know or if it focused on what a person needs to do to become more like Jesus?* If someone felt they were already growing in discipleship more from a belief focus, but needed to grow more with a behavior focus, they would answer in the 1–4 range. If someone felt they were already growing in a more behavior-focused discipleship manner, but needed to grow in a more belief-focused manner, they would answer in the 6–10 range.

Gathered-Sent

While this category does apply to individuals, it is perhaps most helpful for assessing the culture of a local church as a whole. This category can also serve as a summary of sorts of the previous three categories.

In gathered discipleship settings, disciples grow through centralized, organized opportunities on their turf. Discipleship here occurs when believers come together in intentional ways to strengthen one another. The orientation here is toward planned endeavors that are usually conducted through the life of the inherited church body. Those in gathered settings benefit, usually, from the resources and organized activities offered in local church settings (such as church facilities, paid staff, and professional teaching). Activities such as organized Bible studies, regular Sunday morning worship, and weekly life groups would fall under this category. Elements such as choirs, paid pastors, and updated sanctuary spaces become possible in gathered discipleship settings.

In sent discipleship settings, discipleship happens when God's people go out into the world to meet people on their turf in order to be a witness to the love and power of Jesus in more decentralized ways. Practices such as starting dinner churches, meeting in nursing homes, gathering in gyms, joining for worship on mountains, celebrating in tattoo parlors, sharing around swing dancing, and organizing optional faith discussions in local schools would all be ways to focus on sent forms of discipleship.

A key question to ask in this tension to determine where one is on the scale of 1 (gathered) to 10 (sent) would be: *Would discipleship be more effective if people had more time to connect and encourage one another or if they took more time to connect and bless people who do not currently know Jesus?* If someone felt they were already growing in a more gathered discipleship manner but needed to grow in a more sent manner, they would answer in the 1–4 range. If someone felt they were already growing in a more sent discipleship manner but needed to grow in a more gathered discipleship manner, they would answer in the 6–10 range.

Navigating the Already/Not Yet Tension

As indicated earlier, part of the beauty of this approach is that under each area of tension, individuals can simultaneously identify and celebrate which elements of discipleship they are already living into and identify which areas of discipleship they are deficient in. In this way, affirmation and appropriate challenge in discipleship are offered. Individuals are encouraged and confronted with where they need to grow at the same time. Thus, a tension of "already/not yet" is realized.

What emerges, then, is a multilayered approach to a multifaceted problem. When these tensions are applied to each person's unique gifts, talents, and abilities, we discover yet another complete set of layers by which to help each person grow in discipleship. The net result is an approach that can be applied to everyone but yields unique results based on where each person is in his or her faith and discipleship journey, so individuals are both celebrated and appropriately challenged in ways specific to them.

One other distinguishing element of this process is that this discipleship journey presents a bottom-up rather than top-down approach. In top-down methods, the desired outcomes are already known and pursued. For example, maybe a church is hoping to find more youth volunteers and choir members. Many discipleship journeys are then set up to encourage people to volunteer to fill these slots, whether it is a proper fit for them or not. Under this model announcements and mass communication are utilized in order to fill predetermined needs.

In bottom-up approaches, everyone is challenged to deeper discipleship (that part is nonnegotiable). But how they are challenged will vary depending on where each individual is in her or his faith journey. As a result, each individual will be challenged to grow in ways that are uniquely applicable in his or her life. The good news here is that, because the approach and challenge will meet individuals exactly where they are in their faith journeys, individuals have a greater likelihood to respond in their next discipleship step because it is relevant to them. The challenge is that how those individuals respond may or may not address a known church need. Leaders must learn to become okay with this approach by trusting in the concept of the Body of Christ, as 1 Corinthians 12 describes. In the Body of Christ, each person plays a part to live out faith and faithfulness based on how God has designed them and in the process all needs are eventually met. In this way, the focus becomes authentic discipleship development rather than manufactured volunteer sign-ups.

One final word to offer about these tensions: While key questions are involved in each of these tensions, there is one particular question that can—and should—be asked of all of them once one figures out which side of a discipleship tension one is on. That question is: *How can these discipleship tensions help you to become more like Jesus?* To be more precise, how can the opposite side of the discipleship continuum that you are on be used to catalyze you to more fruitful discipleship? This one question provides significant opportunity for every individual who goes through each discipleship tension to consider what new discipleship opportunity they should most live into. This question can also be visited on a repeated basis as a way of helping individuals continue to grow in their ever-developing discipleship journeys.

Part of the beauty of this approach is that it allows individuals to consider where they currently are in their discipleship journeys, and then simultaneously points out what step might be next. This approach also allows for a communal sense of discernment as individuals hear from the rest of the group on what the group sees as strengths and opportunities for that individual to live into in the discipleship journey.

One other communal benefit of these tensions is how they begin to offer clues to how the church as a whole needs to move in order to be a more faithful church. For example, if many of the people in Disciple's Journey are thriving in going deep in their faith, but are not reaching new people in the faith, the church should consider one set of actions. But if many in Disciple's Journey are reaching many new people in the faith but not spending any time in deeper faith formation, the church should consider another set of focus points moving forward. Once again we see a multilayered solution offered to a multifactorial problem! Because of these realities, most of the time spent in step 3 is working with each person who is a part of it by helping them discern their next faithful step while they share in the identified practices of step 3. In this way individuals feel seen and affirmed by the group and also realize how they can grow in their discipleship.

Individuals who complete step 3, in particular, are viewed as being at a point when they are ready to become influencers and leaders of others. Individuals who finish step 3 have demonstrated they are familiar with the content and practices of the church DNA and are at a place where they are prepared to encourage others in their faith journey.

DISCIPLE'S JOURNEY STEP 4

Finally, in step 4, we invite people into various informal, ongoing relationships. In this step individuals are encouraged to enter into apprenticeship with a mentor in the area of ministry they have felt called to, participate in a resourcing experience, or share in some combination of the two. These individuals are now understood as key leaders and influencers. The focus here is creating a multiplying effect as ultimately new people are introduced into faith through the discipleship of those in this fourth step. Here we seek to ignite and unleash individuals into their formative and generative callings in the most practical of ways.

THE ONGOING DISCIPLESHIP JOURNEY

This discipleship approach, admittedly, is messy because it involves responding appropriately with each individual and where that person is in her or his own discipleship experience. Thus, this discipleship journey is not a static one—and that is part of its significance and effectiveness! Jim Collins talks about the power of the flywheel.[4] The concept of the flywheel is that in order for a culture to change, certain focus points, activities, and ways of doing things must be done over and over and over. Collins gives the image of pushing a rock up a hill. To get the rock to complete even one rotation takes a tremendous amount of effort. However, once one is able to complete a few rotations of the rock, get it to the summit, and let it start to go down the other side, the rotations become much easier as the momentum picks up.

AUTHENTIC DISCIPLESHIP IS NOT STATIC.

In similar fashion, the discipleship process being described here is one that occurs on a continual, repeated, annual basis. Knowing that people have busy lives, that the Spirit moves at dif-

---

4. Jim Collins, *Good to Great: Why Some Companies Make the Leap and Others Don't* (New York: HarperBusiness, 2001).

ferent times, and that circumstances change, this journey is offered in such a way as to allow people to engage when and as they are most ready. Some people may take steps 1 and 2 almost immediately and then take years to get to step 3. Others may take step 1, then wait a few years until step 2, and never get to step 3. Still others may go through all four steps as quickly as possible. With each rotation of the discipleship journey in a local church setting, the culture shifts a little more to allow for dynamic discipleship to flourish in the church culture as a whole.

The easiest way to envision how this discipleship journey plays out in a local church setting is to consider what a normal year might look like. The first step of connection in Disciple's Journey step 1 (five sessions) usually occurs three times a year—in the fall, the winter, and early spring (but you can adjust this to the needs of your setting). Then step 2 (six sessions), focused on discovery, occurs each fall. Step 3 (eight sessions depending on how many are participating), focused on embracing gifts, occurs each spring. Then in step 4 folks share in informal, overlapping cohort experiences as they move through their three-year pilgrimage. This approach is both intentional and organic . . . both structured and flexible. It is a wonderfully messy tension to navigate!

DISCIPLE'S JOURNEY—IMPACT

We were unsure what results this type of discipleship paradigm might yield. What we have discovered is that each step requires a greater commitment. Therefore each step does filter out individuals over time, but it also invites those who want to live into greater fruitfulness in discipleship to do just that. The net result is discipleship multiplication that stems more from discipleship quality than from discipleship quantity. We have discovered that

God does a lot (and impacts a lot of people) with a few, just like Jesus changed the world through His investment in the original twelve disciples. We are okay if there are only a few who ever get to the fourth step of our Disciple's Journey each year, because we believe (and now we have seen!) that they will make a powerful, multiplying difference through their full commitment.

Since we are not seeking to fill particular volunteer quotas, we never know what might emerge as people embrace their gifts and live them out. However, we have been thrilled to see who God has raised up through deeper discipleship. We have lived into the reality of the Body of Christ in new ways as we have trusted God to lead people to the right areas of ministry rather than focusing on where we might want them to go. This approach has led to much more vitality and ministry involvement than when we simply tried to fill slots.

Just a few examples of what forms of more mature discipleship have looked like for those who have engaged in Disciple's Journey:

- A nursing home Fresh Expressions leader
- A director for a Code Blue homeless shelter in the church facility
- A Disciple's Journey step 1 facilitator
- A worship facilitator for a worship service
- A Bible study teacher for individuals at a dinner church
- A youth leader of high school guys
- A children's ministry advocate and resource creator
- A teacher who has created multiple church-wide fall kickoff devotionals
- A prayer warrior who has been led to engage the entire church in multiple church-wide prayer initiatives

It has been thrilling to watch these individuals grow in their discipleship in these ways. Before we began exploring the new life to be found in the tensions of this discipleship journey, we (or I!) had assumed that people were either not serious about their discipleship or that our local church simply did not have individuals with these discipleship gifts.

What we have since discovered is that the people were there and the gifts were there. But a culture that allowed people to both identify and then be empowered to live into more mature discipleship was what was missing. The biggest barrier was not busyness, a secular culture, passivity, hurriedness, or even apathy . . . the biggest barrier was a church culture that was not navigating the discipleship tensions in a relevant, authentic, ongoing way.

Perhaps the same is true for you.

INTERVENING QUESTIONS AND EXERCISES

1. What sticks out to you about the following quotation? Discuss it with some other people. What strikes you? What steps can you take to avoid drifting when it comes to discipleship?

"Nobody drifts into a committed, growing relationship with Christ. Nobody wakes up one day and says, 'I'm not sure how it happened, but without really knowing it, I am a lot like Jesus in every area of my life.'
—J.R. Briggs

2. In the tension of formal and informal discipleship, which side comes more naturally to you as a church? as individuals? Which one is more challenging? Why? How can one side help influence the other in your setting?

3. Ask your leadership team to list all the elements of formal discipleship going on in your local setting.

4. Ask your leadership team to list all of the elements of informal discipleship going on in your local setting.

5. Rank your level of formal discipleship on a scale of 1 to 10 (1 being low on the scale for discipleship and 10 being very high).

6. Rank your level of informal discipleship on a scale of 1 to 10 (1 being low on the scale for discipleship and 10 being very high).

7. What is the primary barrier occurring at each level of discipleship?

8. What would it look like to create an ongoing/repeating cycle of discipleship opportunities?

9. What is a next step you can take to be intentional in rediscovering discipleship?

   • Do you have a version of the first step of Disciple's Journey? Is it clear to people?

   • Do you have a version of the second step of Disciple's Journey? Is it clear to people?

   • How can you create a version of the third and fourth steps of Disciple's Journey?

10. Is intentional discipleship owned by one or a few in your church? Or is the whole church aligned around discipleship? How can you bring more alignment with the whole church?

For an overview of what this tension between formal and informal discipleship can look like in a local setting, along with how it has impacted people in their discipleship journeys, check out this video: https://firstchurch.cc/home/disciplesjourney/.

CROSS THE DISCIPLESHIP CHASM: WHEN TENSION LEADS TO NEW DISCIPLESHIP LIFE

Up to this point, I have laid out an adaptive approach to discipleship based on discipleship tensions as discovered through a process of observing, interpreting, and intervening. Or at least this adaptive discipleship approach has been laid out in theory. But what happens beyond theory? What happens in real life? on the ground? in ministry? How do these tensions yield new discipleship life for individuals and in church cultures as a whole?

I want to provide a number of practical examples, firsthand, of how we have witnessed new discipleship life as a result of the embracing of the tensions laid out in this book. We will explore some examples of individuals who have gone through Disciple's Journey and how the discipleship tensions yielded new life in their lives and impacted the lives of others.

A FRAMEWORK FOR MAKING THE JOURNEY ACROSS THE DISCIPLESHIP CHASM

When it comes to individuals participating in Disciple's Journey, everyone follows a similar path within the framework of observing, interpreting, and intervening. However, each individual also experiences a unique manifestation of more mature discipleship engagement based on her or his unique wiring and journey with God.

The framework for each person involves the following:

In Disciple's Journey step 2, each participant shares in a series of observation exercises such as:

- Naming top passions they have
- Spiritual gift inventories
- APEST (Apostle, Prophet, Evangelist, Shepherd, Teacher) inventories
- Strengths inventories such as StrengthsFinder by Tom Rath
- Identifying involvement in any previous ministries

Additionally, participants in step 2 begin to observe and reflect on an introduction to the tensions that have been identified. These tensions include:

- Formal-Informal
- Deep-New
- Belief-Behavior
- Gathered-Sent

In Disciple's Journey step 3, participants focus more on interpretation and intervention.

INTERPRETATION OF THE TENSIONS

Formal-Informal

Formal discipleship is recognized as organized opportunities to grow as a Christian, usually offered on a regular or scheduled basis. Informal discipleship is recognized as interactions that seek to help people become more like Jesus and that result from organic relationships and opportunities. The key interpretive question here is: *Would discipleship be more effective if it became more intentionally structured or if it became more available/responsive?*

Deep-New

Deep discipleship results in existing believers becoming more like Jesus. New discipleship results in new believers in Christ. The key interpretive question here is: *Would discipleship be more effective if it focused on strengthening existing believers in Christ or if it focused on reaching new believers in Christ?*

Belief-Behavior

Discipleship focused on belief seeks to foster transformation of the mind by imparting knowledge and engaging with the scripture. Discipleship focused on behavior seeks to equip a person to become more Christlike in action. The key interpretive question here is: *Would discipleship be more effective if it focused on what a person needs to know or if it focused on what a person needs to do to become more like Jesus?*

Gathered (Centralized)-Sent (Decentralized)

Gathered discipleship happens when believers come together in centralized, intentional ways to strengthen one another (worship, life groups, etc.). Sent discipleship occurs when God's people go out into the world to meet people on their turf (and plan to stay there!) in order to be a witness to the love and power of Jesus in decentralized ways. The key interpretive question here is: *Would discipleship be more effective if people had more time to connect and encourage one another or if they took more time to connect with and bless people who currently do not know Jesus?*

Living into the Tensions

As people begin to recognize and interpret where they are in the midst of each of these tensions, they then ask one final, key, interpretive question: *How can the opposite side of the discipleship continuum that you are on be used to imaginatively stimulate and catalyze you to a more mature discipleship?*

By asking this one key question in each of the identified tension areas there is the recognition that new life is fostered by embracing the tension found in moving toward the end of the spectrum that one is not currently on. In this way, individuals can be affirmed in where they are doing well in their discipleship journey and also discover where they need to grow.

For example, if someone recognizes they are doing great in formal discipleship through Bible study, personal devotion, and regular worship, this is to be celebrated. At the same time if that same person recognizes they are not engaging in their faith in everyday life in workplaces or with friends, or other third-space places, they would be challenged to grow in this area of discipleship in their lives.

Or if someone recognizes they are always talking with others about the faith and sharing the good news of Christ with people who do not know Jesus, this is to be celebrated. At the same time, if this same person recognizes they are always on the go and rarely take time to go deep with Jesus through quiet time, solitude, study, meditation, and prayer, then they would be challenged to grow in this area of discipleship in their lives.

As each person navigates these interpretive tensions, they discover if they need to be more structured or less structured in their discipleship. They begin to understand if they need to be meeting more new people in the faith or dive deeper in their faith. They start to realize if they need to think into their faith more or act into their faith more. Overall, individuals begin to comprehend if their discipleship orientation needs to be more gathered in focus or more sent in focus.

As this interpretive work is applied in each discipleship tension, new life emerges precisely through the tensions. In this way, bridges—new ways—into more mature discipleship are created that were not present before.

Once an individual interprets where they are in the midst of each discipleship tension, then they can begin to apply these interpretations to the observations made in connection with their passions, gifts, and strengths. This application then points the way to what discipleship interventions each individual needs to take.

Let's examine a few case studies of those who have crossed the discipleship chasm.

CASE STUDY #1: MEGAN (MOM OF TWO YOUNG BOYS)[5]

Megan observed that some of her strengths included empathy, relating, learning, arranging, and developing (as defined in Rath's StrengthsFinder).

Megan also observed that she has spiritual gifts of hospitality, wisdom, and teaching while discovering that her top APEST gift was teacher.

Beyond this, Megan observed that she has a deep passion for prayer.

When Megan interpreted each discipleship tension she realized that the areas of discipleship she was doing well in were the more formal, deep, belief, and gathered ways. This reality was cel-

---

5. Names of individuals mentioned in all the case studies have been changes for the sake of anonymity.

ebrated with Megan. Conversely Megan realized more growth was needed in her discipleship life in more informal, newer, behavior-oriented, sent ways.

Megan then asked, in light of her gifts, passions, and strengths: "How can the opposite side of the discipleship continuums that I am on be used to imaginatively stimulate and catalyze me to a more mature discipleship?"

When Megan did this, questions such as the following began to emerge:

With the deep-new tension: "How can Megan reach/influence new people in the faith?"

With the belief-behavior tension: "How can Megan put more faith practices into her life?"

Since prayer was a deep passion for Megan, and teaching was a strong orientation, the more specific question arose: "How might prayer and teaching be mixed together in an action-oriented way to reach new people?"

Megan is deeply empathetic and is strong in arranging many different pieces while developing others by challenging them to grow into their potential (as her StrengthsFinder revealed).

So, by applying the interpretations of the discipleship tensions to the observations of her abilities and passions, Megan was led to consider the following interventions:

One: Wrote prayers for each of the forty days leading up to the launch of a fall kickoff for the entire church. The prayers focused on encouraging people to reengage or join in life groups, studies, service opportunities, faith opportunities, etc. for the first time. These prayers were emailed to anyone in the church who wanted them so that as many as possible could be involved in the overall prayer initiative.

Two: Galvanized a prayer movement for a significant discernment process the entire church went through.

Three: Led a Lenten prayer initiative for the congregation that reached new people who had never before been involved.

Not only has Megan's own discipleship journey grown in this time, but these new discipleship steps have impacted many new people in new ways for their discipleship growth. It has been beautiful!

Perhaps most encouraging of all, this journey into the discipleship tensions has been a joy for Megan in her own walk of faith and not a burden. As Megan herself has shared:

> It has been such a blessing to take this [prayer initiative] project in hand. I have really loved the amount of learning and reflection and growth that I personally received, and I have also loved hearing from people far and wide that also enjoyed their Lent journey. I had many private messages and ten people just this past week stopped me. It is really incredible how many of them say that they learned so much about themselves and grew deeper in faith. The testimonies are so awesome. I had people in Florida, Delaware, Virginia, Georgia, and Texas and beyond connect because people were sharing that I did not know about. So cool!

Then Megan shared, "I'm praying on where to be led!"

Do you hear the new discipleship life? For Megan and others?

CASE STUDY #2: KEN (RETIRED BUSINESS OWNER)

Ken is a man in his seventies. Ken observed that some of his gifts include being visionary, organizing, being a leader, encouragement, and bringing alignment.

Ken also observed that he has spiritual gifts of faith, administration, and hospitality. Ken's top APEST gift was apostle.

Beyond this, Ken observed that he has a deep passion for mission and outreach to new people not in the church.

When Ken interpreted each discipleship tension he realized that the areas of discipleship he was doing well in were the informal, new, behavior, and sent areas. This reality was celebrated with Ken. Conversely Ken realized more growth was needed in his discipleship life in more formal, deep, belief, and gathered ways.

Ken then asked, in light of his gifts, passions, and strengths: "How can the opposite side of the discipleship continuums that I am on be used to imaginatively stimulate and catalyze me to a more mature discipleship?"

When Ken did this, questions such as the following began to emerge:

With formal-informal tension: "How can Ken through his relationships invite people into more formal faith opportunities?"

With the belief-behavior tension: "How can Ken help others think more about their belief in Christ to drive their actions?"

Since reaching new people is such a passion for Ken, and he had such a strong apostolic impulse, the more specific question arose: "How might Ken use his apostolic gift to reach new people while providing grounding opportunities for faith reflection?"

By applying the interpretations of the discipleship tensions to the observations of his abilities and passions, Ken was led to consider the following interventions:

One: With his wife, Ken launched a Code Blue warming center in the gathered church facility. In connection with this service Ken and his wife have brought many of the guests to formal worship services and offered a Bible study for the guests.

Two: Serving as the chairperson of the governance board of the gathered local church to help it take more sent-oriented actions.

Three: Helped launch a dinner church experience in a third space in the community.

Again, not only has Ken's own discipleship journey grown in this time, but these new discipleship steps have impacted many new people in new ways for their discipleship growth. It has been beautiful!

As Ken himself has shared:

> We dreamed about ways that we might serve the homeless population in our community. Eventually this effort led to what became known as the Code Blue shelter in our church facility. Since its inception over 80 volunteers have served as overnight hosts with over 240 men, women, and children occupying over 4000 beds, and over 4000 meals have been served, all for the purpose of sharing the love and hope offered only by Jesus Christ. We envisioned, founded, and have led this and other ministry initiatives because we have felt personally called by Christ and sent to serve because above all else we love Jesus. Through them [those we have served] we've experienced joyful mountaintop times where we sat humbly next to our God and we've experienced times in the desert where we experienced frustration, anxiety, and sometimes even fear. As apostles we would not change a thing . . . the more we humble ourselves to serve the more we are blessed.

Do you hear Ken's excitement as he grows in his own discipleship and impacts the discipleship of others?

CASE STUDY #3: KYLE (DAD OF THREE GRADE SCHOOL KIDS)

Kyle observed that some of his strengths included context, responsibility, discipline, being strategic, and consistency.

Kyle also observed that he has spiritual gifts of faith, teaching, and administration. His top APEST gift was teacher.

Beyond this, Kyle observed that he has a deep passion for youth and teaching by taking difficult concepts and making them simple. Kyle also identified that he is very logical and likes to encourage.

When Kyle interpreted each discipleship tension he realized that the areas of discipleship where he was doing well were the informal, deep, belief, and gathered areas. This reality was celebrated with Kyle. Conversely, Kyle realized that more growth was needed in his life in more formal, new, behavior, and sent ways.

Kyle then asked, in light of his gifts, passions, and strengths: "How can the opposite side of the discipleship continuums that I am on be used to imaginatively stimulate and catalyze me to a more mature discipleship?"

When Kyle did this, questions such as the following began to emerge:

With formal-informal: "How can Kyle be intentional in being more formal in his faith walk?"

With the belief-behavior tension: "What action can Kyle take to put belief into practice?"

Since teaching was a deep passion for Kyle, and teaching was a strong APEST orientation, a more specific question arose: "How might Kyle use his teaching giftedness to encourage others in a logical, organized way?"

By applying the interpretations of the discipleship tensions to the observations of his abilities and passions, Kyle was led to consider the following interventions:

One: Co-wrote a congregation-wide devotion that had never been done before in line with a church fall kickoff. This endeavor has continued each year since Kyle helped start it.

Two: Led a children's ministry tween Bible study that had not existed.

Three: Participated in vacation Bible school.

Four: Served as a life-group leader.

Once more, not only has Kyle's own discipleship journey grown in this time, but these new discipleship steps have impacted many new people in new ways for their discipleship growth.

While Kyle has been challenged into more mature discipleship, Kyle has discovered his own growth as a disciple. Kyle shares:

> The ministries I am involved with at church—the children's ministry and fall kickoff especially—both stem out of what I perceive to be my strengths but also my passions. However, my involvement in each has occurred for very different reasons. I love teaching and I love watching and encouraging other people to grow in their faith and walk with the Lord. Through the fall kickoff, I enjoy knowing that the devotions I helped to create will create meaningful study of scripture and will elicit stimulating thoughts and small-group conversations, which hopefully encourages people in their faith. I hope it helps them create a stronger understanding of God, and ultimately draws them closer to Christ. Furthermore, my love of researching and continued personal learning means that I, too, am drawing closer to God as I personally study while creating the devotional content for others.

Kyle had needed to grow in more formal discipleship. As he embraced that tension, notice how the focus of his action steps involved a more formal approach. As Kyle is growing in his discipleship he is helping others grow as well.

CASE STUDY #4: JUDY (RECENTLY RETIRED GRANDMOTHER)

Judy observed that some of her top strengths include being a connector, developer, and relator along with consistency and harmony.

Judy also observed that she has spiritual gifts of faith, giving, and hospitality, and that her top APEST gifts were evangelist and teacher.

Beyond this, Judy observed that she has a deep passion for connection with family and friends and studying God's Word.

When Judy interpreted each discipleship tension she realized that the areas of discipleship she was doing well in were the formal, deep, behavior, and sent ways. This reality was celebrated with Judy. Conversely Judy realized more growth was needed in her discipleship life in more informal, new, belief, and gathered ways.

Judy then asked, in light of her gifts, passions, and strengths: "How can the opposite side of the discipleship continuums that I am on be used to imaginatively stimulate and catalyze me to a more mature discipleship?"

When Judy did this, questions such as the following began to emerge:

With the deep-new tension: "How can Judy be intentional to reach or connect to new people?"

With the belief-behavior tension: "How can Judy help others think more about their belief in Christ?"

Since evangelism and teaching, along with connecting, were deep passions for Judy, the more specific question arose: "How might Judy use her evangelizing and teaching gifts to connect with new people in a more gathered way?" *Notice here how the emphasis in the question leans into areas where Judy needed to grow in her own discipleship.* Another question that arose for Judy was: "How can Judy help develop people into deeper faith?"

By once again applying the interpretations of the discipleship tensions to the observations of her abilities and passions, Judy was led to consider the following intervention steps:

One: Became the primary facilitator of the Disciple's Journey step 1 experience. In taking this step, Judy is connecting brand new people into the life of the church, and she is doing this in a more gathered way where she helps people focus on belief. Additionally Judy is doing this through her passions and gifts of sharing the good news (evangelism) and teaching each new Disciple's Journey step 1 group as those individuals enter into the life of the church. It should also be noted here that because Judy has taken this step of discipleship in her life, a pastor or staff person is not needed to facilitate this very important connection.

Two: Serving on the church's primary governance structure to help continue to foster the sent orientation for the church as a whole.

Three: Serving in the church office on a weekly basis to be able to serve, greet, and connect with church individuals and community individuals who come in.

Yet again, not only has Judy's own discipleship journey grown in this time, but these new discipleship steps have impacted many new people in new ways for their discipleship journey. Judy has helped individuals grow in formative ways while also being more deeply connected into the life of the congregation.

Judy's joy and passion are palpable as she shares about how her discipleship growth has personally impacted her.

> My faith journey began many years ago. I learned to love the
> Lord through the witness of others, prayer, Bible study, and be-

longing to a faith community. The Lord has spoken to me in many ways. I have heard God's call in the night and on many walks. My desire to follow the command to "go and make disciples" and to "love one another" has led me to the ministries I am currently involved in. I am absolutely thrilled to use my genuine caring, practical perspective, and spiritual skills in the ministries that I lead. All these skills come from God. I am humbled to serve Him and others through the initiatives I am called to.

Megan, Ken, Kyle, and Judy are all at different stages of life. They all have different skills, abilities, and passions. Yet as they have embraced the discipleship tensions identified herein and applied them through the observing, interpreting, and intervening framework, new pathways of discipleship have emerged in their lives, and therefore in the lives of others. These are normal individuals in the midst of all of the challenges that every local church faces who are experiencing pathways into new discipleship life that did not exist before. Their stories are both inspiring and instructive. Their discipleship journeys are helping me in mine. I hope they help you in yours.

A FINAL WORD

That day on our family vacation on the swinging bridges was a day I and my family will never forget. I had never experienced anything quite like it. It was simultaneously old (I had been on plenty of bridges) and new (but never walked among treetops before). It felt safe (there were many giant pillars holding the bridge in place) and scary (we really were swinging hundreds of feet in the air). Only by embracing both the old and the new, along with the safe and the scary, were we able to experience the fullness of the adventure. Only by literally walking the tension of the bridge itself were we able to go where we had never gone before, into what would otherwise be impossible.

Discipleship in Christ is like that. In the faith we are held safely but always called into the unknown. We both feel comfortable and are always stretched beyond ourselves. And then only as we follow Jesus—the true Way—can we discover new life and discipleship where there was none before. When we can learn to embrace the holy tension found in Jesus, we will discover new ways forward in our discipleship, even in the forest of challenges in which we find ourselves.

While we still have a ways to go in our local setting in regard to discipleship (don't we always?), we have been encouraged by the discipleship maturity we have seen as a result of embracing the discipleship tensions through observing, interpreting, and intervening. We have seen a shift in our overall discipleship culture. We believe we are making progress in our discipleship because of two key elements.

First, there is now congregational alignment around discipleship. In our setting we have three core characteristics that we talk about in relation to who we are. One of those characteristics is "rugged discipleship." By focusing on discipleship as an entire congregation we stand a much better chance of making progress in our discipleship with individuals. We use the words "rugged discipleship" not just as an aspirational descriptor but as a north star toward which to move.

Second, we are slowly learning to integrate and synchronize how we "do" church at all levels. Thus we expect our staff to help recruit new people into our Disciple's Journey while also modeling mentoring relationships in their own lives. We expect our laity to do the same. We expect that church life will be sensitive to fostering our discipleship journeys. We invite people through formal means (verbal announcements, mass emails, etc.) as well as through much more organic means (personal invitations and shoulder taps). In these ways the Disciple's Journey DNA is seeping into our culture as a whole. Maybe it can for you as well.

I invite you into a new way forward by traversing the changing landscape through discipleship tensions that are anchored in God's foundational truths and practices.

We are discovering the power and significance of how such a discipleship journey can lead to deeper discipleship and greater church vitality.

You can too.

SCAN HERE to learn more about Invite Press, a premier publishing imprint created to invite people to a deeper faith and living relationship with Jesus Christ.